THE ULT1MATE SUCCESS
SECRET

"Flying around all day just won't cut it—sooner or later, you're going to have to fight some evil."

© Charles Barsotti/The New Yorker Collection/www.cartoonbank.com

Is it possible that there is one single, super-powerful secret of success of far greater importance than all others?

THE ULT1MATE SUCCESS
SECRET

BEN GLASS
www.BenGlassLaw.com

DAN S. KENNEDY
www.DanKennedy.com

Copyright © 2005, 2011 by Dan S. Kennedy

First edition published 2005. Second edition 2012.

ALL RIGHTS ARE RESERVED. No part of this publication may be reproduced or transmitted in any form or by any means, mechanical or electronic, including photocopying and recording, or by any information storage and retrieval system, without permission in writing from the Publisher.

Published by: Kennedy Inner Circle, Inc.
15433 N. Tatum Blvd., #104, Phoenix, AZ 85032
Licensed for reprint to certain authorized additional publishers.

Authorized Publisher:
BenGlassLaw/Great Legal Marketing
3915 Old Lee Highway
Suite 22-B
Fairfax, VA 22030

DISCLAIMER AND/OR LEGAL NOTICES:

While all attempts have been made to verify information provided in this publication, neither the Authors nor the Publisher assumes any responsibility for errors, inaccuracies or omissions. Any slights of people or organizations are unintentional.

This publication is not intended for use as a source of legal or accounting advice. The Publisher wants to stress that the information contained herein may be subject to varying state and/or local laws or regulations. All users are advised to retain competent counsel to determine what state and/or local laws or regulations may apply to the user's particular business.

The purchaser or reader of this publication assumes responsibility for the use of these materials and information. Adherence to all applicable laws and regulations, both advertising and all other aspects of doing business in the United States or any other jurisdiction is the sole responsibility of the purchaser or reader. The Authors and Publisher assume no responsibility or liability whatsoever on the behalf of any purchaser or reader of these materials.

PRINTED IN THE UNITED STATES OF AMERICA

Table of Contents

A Favorite Story 7

Introduction – Ben Glass 11

Introduction – Dan Kennedy 13

About The Authors 19

Chapter 1 – Ben Glass 21

Chapter 2 – Dan Kennedy 23

Chapter 3 – Ben Glass 31

Chapter 4 – Dan Kennedy 35

Chapter 5 – Ben Glass 49

Chapter 6 – Dan Kennedy 53

Chapter 7 – Ben Glass 69

Chapter 8 – Dan Kennedy 73

Chapter 9 – Ben Glass 85

Chapter 10 – Dan Kennedy 89

Chapter 11 – Ben Glass 97

Chapter 12 – Dan Kennedy 99

Chapter 13 – Ben Glass 107

Chapter 14 – Dan Kennedy.............................. 109

Chapter 15 – Ben Glass................................ 115

Chapter 16 – Dan Kennedy.............................. 117

Chapter 17 – Ben Glass................................ 125

Chapter 18 – Dan Kennedy.............................. 127

Chapter 19 – Ben Glass................................ 137

Chapter 20 – Dan Kennedy.............................. 139

Chapter 21 – Ben Glass................................ 145

Chapter 22 – Dan Kennedy.............................. 149

Chapter 23 – Ben Glass................................ 155

Chapter 24 – Dan Kennedy.............................. 157

Chapter 25 – Ben Glass................................ 173

Chapter 26 – Dan Kennedy.............................. 175

Epilogue... 183

About The Authors.................................... 187

About This Book...................................... 191

A Favorite Story

The much revered, very wise, aged rabbi is on his deathbed, his rabbinical students gathered for the deathwatch, arranged with the smartest of the students at the rabbi's head, the next smartest second, and so on, down to the pitied dunce of the class, at the foot of the bed. As it becomes increasingly apparent that the old rabbi was soon to depart, his best student leaned over and whispered, "Before you leave us, could you please, finally, **give us THE secret of life itself**, great master teacher, sir?"

After a few moments of thought, with considerable effort, the rabbi managed to croak out, "Life is like a river."

The honored student turned to the one next to him and said," The master said 'life is like a river.' Pass it down." And so each student in turn passed the wisdom down to the next. But the dunce said, "Hey, wait a minute, life is like a river? What does that mean? Ask him what he means by that."

Ashamed and tentative, each student passed the question back up the line. The best student again leaned over and said, "I'm sorry, master teacher, but the dunce, down at the end, he does not understand. He wants to know: what do you mean?—life is like a river."

With every ounce of strength remaining in his dying, frail body, the rabbi managed these last words: "Okay, so it's *not* like a river."

"A Lobster When Left High And Dry Among The Rocks, Has Not Instinct And Energy Enough To Work His Way Back To The Sea, But Waits For The Sea To Come To Him. If It Does Not Come, He Remains Where He Is And Dies, Although The Slightest Effort Would Enable Him To Reach The Waves, Which Are Perhaps within a yard of him.

The world is full of human lobsters: men stranded on the rocks of indecision and procrastination, who, instead of putting forth their own energies, are waiting for some grand billow of good fortune to set them afloat."

–Dr. Orrison Swett Marden

Introduction – Ben Glass

I am honored to co-author *The Ultimate Success Secret* with my friend and mentor, Dan Kennedy. For years I struggled with building and maintaining my personal injury law firm. Somewhere around 2003 I joined "Planet Dan." Here I found ideas and tactics that would help make me ultra successful in a very, very competitive marketplace (just check out Google listings for "attorneys" or "lawyers!"). Contrary to what most people believe, most lawyers are not rich. In fact, most work a crushing number of hours in a pressure-filled world and don't make a ton of money. More importantly, many have traded away their families, their health and sometimes their own lives for "success." Dan Kennedy not only introduced me to new marketing and business building ideas, but he also showed me an entirely different mindset. He encouraged me to stop thinking like a lawyer; to buck industry norms; and to begin thinking like a real business owner.

I have been writing about "success" for several years now, drawing on not only my own experience that of others. My contribution to this book with Dan Kennedy is a collection of "Success" articles that have appeared in my newsletter. Each of the articles includes the date when it first appeared.

THE ULTIMATE SUCCESS SECRET

If you have never heard of Dan Kennedy before and like the ideas you find in this book, I encourage you to go to DanKennedyAndBenGlass.com to get instant access.

If you are an attorney and are tired of handing your wallet over to the marketing vultures (i.e. Internet vendors, pay-per-click thieves, and print and TV salespeople), the go buy my marketing book for lawyers, available at GreatLegalMarketingBook.com. We have the answers to your questions.

Introduction – Dan Kennedy

What You Will Discover In This Book

Why have Ben Glass and I written a book with such an audacious title?

It sometimes seems like only yesterday that I was a punk kid with big ideas, adding gray to my hair to try and look a little older. I certainly do not have *that* problem now. I could stand to take some of the gray out. After a speaking engagement not long ago, my friend Lee Milteer observed that my groupies seem to be getting a lot older. Anyway, I feel like I've stacked up enough expensive experience to justify committing some opinions about "the ultimate success secret" to paper. I have gone from broke to well off; from severe struggle to peaks of success in not one but three professional fields; and, along the way, I have had the good fortune of working with, hanging out with quite a number of exceptionally successful people from business, sports, entertainment. Famous people, like Joan Rivers, who started over after her husband's suicide and her loss of her career, working for $500.00 a week on *"Hollywood Squares"*, pronounced a washed up has-been by her own agent; who re-invented her career and her life with courage and determination. And non-famous people, like Gladdie Gill, a 50+ year old school teacher living uncomplainingly with Hodgkin's disease; on her summer vacations, climbing mountains, traversing Alaska in a jeep; at home, taking care of every imaginable orphaned animal; at school, defying dullard administrators to give her students the richest imaginable learning experiences, thus earning the support of an entire community of parents and kids, and having a truly lasting impact on many lives. I have had the privilege of working closely with a great many "from scratch" entrepreneurs like Ben who've built empires, extraordinarily successful salespeople, top executives, top speakers. I have quite literally been surrounded by and immersed in success for years. And I'm a good observer. I have not let this go to waste.

It is impossible to count the number of authors, researchers, psychologists, "motivational gurus", etc. who have been fascinated by the question of what causes some people to be successful and others to fail. We know it is not "environment", as some liberals insist; it cannot be, because out of the very worst environments come fabulously successful individuals, repetitively enough not to be passed off as aberration. Blaming external factors, and excusing a person's results because of external factors, is not going to lead anybody to the answer to this question.

In the United States, probably the most famous of authors to have attacked this question thoroughly was Napoleon Hill. His findings are summarized in his best-known book, *Think And Grow Rich*, a bestseller in its time, and, solely thanks to word-of-mouth, a steady seller, surviving and remaining on the fickle bookstore shelves for decades. (If, by some chance you have not read this book, you must.)

In 1917, America's first billionaire, Andrew Carnegie, set Napoleon Hill on a mission to discover the commonalities, the "principles" shared by hundreds of the most exceptional achievers of their time. Eventually, Hill arrived at thirteen such principles. Later, management guru Stephen Covey had a blockbuster best-selling book with his "Seven Habits" of highly successful people. My speaking colleague Zig Ziglar talks about the "Ten Qualities" of successful achievers. Thirteen. Ten. Seven. Pick a number. *Well, I have the audacity to step forward and tell you that I've boiled it down to ONE.*

I changed the question to:

> *Is there one, single secret to success*
> *of such overriding importance that,*
> *if concentrated upon exclusively,*
> *will literally change a person's entire*
> *life experience and results?*
> *If so, what is it?*

That's right—one. I believe that I have identified the one, single, sole "secret of success" universally shared and relied on, above all other success secrets, by all extraordinarily successful individuals. And it is my contention that any person who discovers, accepts, comes to understand, and gives priority, paramount importance to this one secret can and will quickly crate unbelievable breakthroughs in his or her life.

Incidentally, my focus has been quite different than Napoleon Hill's. I have paid a lot less attention to the *thinking* of the successful, and paid a lot more attention to their *behavior*.

In this book, I have NOT come out and simply stated the ultimate secret. Frankly, I could write it down on a 3x5" card. There are several reasons why I haven't done that. First of all, it's darned hard to get $19.95 for a 3x5" card. My accountant, Snarly Stubbyfingers insists that we create things we can sell for profit. (If I refuse, he swears he'll up and leave and he's the only one here with the combination to the safe where we keep the Oreos and the good Scotch.) Second, if I just tell it to you outright, in its shortest form, it lacks useful impact. I've found it is of little use to those I simply tell it to. On the other hand, those who ferret it out for themselves seem to place great value on it and get great value from it. So, I hope you can discover this secret for yourself. It is waiting for you in a number of places in this book.

I don't have any special reason to be overly mysterious, though—so, a clue. The "spark" that drove me to write this book may, in itself, be revealing. A very mundane event got me going. I had been thinking about writing a book on this particular subject for quite some time. I'd been assembling notes on it for a couple years. But there was one little incident that got me to work. On a restless night, late at night, I was thumbing through *TV GUIDE* trying to find something to watch for an hour or so when I noticed this listing:

Movie: ACTION JACKSON!

That name instantly appealed to me. Who was 'Action Jackson'? How did he earn such a dramatic nickname? Well, the movie turned out to be a bad B-picture; a run-of-the-mill cops-and-bad-guys, black exploitation film starring Carl Weathers. I would not recommend the movie. But the hero's name stuck in my mind long after the details of the movie faded. Action Jackson. *That,* I thought at the time, perfectly describes the kind of person who gets the most out of life.

Think about some of the biggest blockbuster movies. *Raiders Of The Lost Ark. Die Hard. Lethal Weapon. Batman. The Fugitive.* Think about the enduring success of the *James Bond* series. Why have these films been such enormous box office moneymakers? I think one of the answers is the dramatic juxtaposition between the movies' always-in-action adventurers and most peoples' comparative slow motion lives. The constant, the universal characteristic of such big screen heroes is their bias for action. And for an hour or two, everybody becomes an Action Jackson, living vicariously through these heroes.

What the Mediocre Majority never learns is that they do not have to settle for living vicariously through others. Anybody can be an Action Jackson—dive headlong into the greatest adventure of all; setting and rapidly accomplishing meaningful, worthwhile goals, meeting fascinating people, visiting exciting places, living an exciting life. Even people who are above-average achievers are often guilty of seeing themselves and their own lives "smaller" than need be.

Well, I am here to tell you that those who live life "large" do share a single, ultimate secret. Through the stories, experiences and examples I've assembled for you, in this book, you can now discover that very secret and get it working for you.

Dan Kennedy

PS: You may have purchased this book on your own, and if so, my thanks and congratulations. But it's also quite likely you received this book as a gift from one of the different business and marketing consultants, advisors, experts or coaches that I've worked with. If that's the case, you should know that the person who gave you this book as a gift is someone who embodies the Ultimate Success Secret through his or her own behavior and business. That person prizes the secret, works at living the secret, and now has invested in passing along the secret to you. If you uncover it and find it valuable, by all means, let them know.

Additional Publisher's Note: this book was first written and published in the early 1990's. Not all references to the author's life or to others in the book have been up-dated. This, in no way, invalidates the timeless message of the book, as you will see.

About The Authors

Ben Glass is a practicing personal injury and medical malpractice attorney in Fairfax, Virginia. He is America's premier authority on "Effective, Ethical and Outside the Box Marketing for Lawyer" (GreatLegalMarketing.com). A nationally recognized personal injury attorney, author and speaker, Ben Glass has written several consumer guides on the law, including *Five Deadly Sins That Can Wreck Your Accident Case* (TheAccidentBook.com), *Why Most Malpractice Victims Never Recover a Dime* (TheMalpracticeBook.com), and *Robbery Without a Gun: Why Your Employer's Long-Term Disability Insurance Policy May Be a Sham* (RobberyWithoutaGun.com). Ben is also the author of *Great Legal Marketing: How Smart Lawyers Think, Behave and Marketing to Get More Clients, Make More Money and Still Get Home in Time for Dinner* (GreatLegalMarketingBook.com).

Dan S. Kennedy is a multi-millionaire serial entrepreneur, sought after and highly paid advisor to entrepreneurs, business owners, CEO's and marketing professionals, and a thought-leader and prolific writer on advertising, marketing, sales, business and success topics. His books have appeared on INC. MAGAZINE'S '100 Best Books' List, Business Week and Amazon bestseller lists, and there has never been a year since 1981 that booksellers' shelves haven't included Dan Kennedy books. Information about his books is available at www.NoBSBooks.com. The sun literally never sets on the reach of the association of entrepreneurs and marketers that has developed around Dan's famous *NO B.S. MARKETING LETTER: Glazer-Kennedy Insider's Circle*™. Information about it is available at www.DanKennedy.com. As a speaker, Dan has frequently addressed audiences of 1,000 to 35,000, and shared the stage with celebrity-entrepreneurs like Donald Trump, Ivanka Trump, Gene Simmons (KISS), Debbi Fields (Mrs. Fields Cookies), George Foreman, and Joan Rivers as well as success and motivational speaking icons Zig Ziglar, Jim Rohn, Brian Tracy and Tom Hopkins. To communicate with Dan directly regarding speaking or consulting engagements, please fax 602-269-3113.

Chapter 1 – Ben Glass

Perfection Is For Dummies

My son, Brian, is studying to take the bar exam this summer. That's right, after three grueling years of law school, a new lawyer-to-be must pass a test in order to get a license. He's taking bar review classes now.

Here's what I told him about the 'mindset' of preparing for the test: *You only have to get a "70" to pass. You don't get any points for perfection.*

The bar exam tests many, many different subjects. What this means for Brian is that once he's scoring around 75 and above in the practice test for a particular subject, he should move on and study a subject he's not yet as proficient in.

What does this mean for you? Too many people delay getting something accomplished in life because they either wait until conditions are perfect to start a project ("one day, when I make enough money, I'll start saving some") or they wait until the project they are doing is completed perfectly until they release it to the world.

How many of you have ever though, "oh, I'd like to write a book sometime, but I just don't have the time to get it all done." I've written 13 books now. You know what? They all had typos and other errors in them the first time we pushed them out the door. You know what else? Errors are fixable. Much better to take on a project and get it completed, than to delay completion until perfection is achieved. Just ask Bill Gates and Microsoft.

The world is full of good ideas that have never seen the light of day because the "owner" of the idea was waiting for "perfect conditions" to act on the idea. All successful people that I know have a bias for action. What's holding you back?

This article first appeared in the July, 2008, edition of the BenGlassLaw newsletter.

Chapter 2 – Dan Kennedy

Take Action To Escape From Prison

Have you ever been inside a real prison? A friend of mine, some years ago, served one year in the Ohio State Penitentiary, and I went to visit him frequently. I can tell you: nothing you see on TV or in the movies can even half prepare you for the shock of the real thing. I don't remember how many times I went inside and back out from behind those prison walls, but the awe, fear, disability and depression I felt never lessened, from the first time to the last. No description I could write could convey the powerlessness that came over me in that environment.

There are millions of people enduring that environment every day.

But that's a small number compared to the many millions of people who might as well be in such a prison for the little joy and satisfaction they're deriving from life. People build their own prisons, incarcerate themselves in them, and make the environments every bit as bleak, stark, depressing and debilitating as the actual penitentiary I visited in Ohio. These peoples' private prisons' block walls are constructed of complaints and resentments, the mortar from excuses, the bars forged from pessimism and procrastination.

We might say that they are locked up in "Pity Prison". Their sentence is indefinite and of their own making. They could walk out as a free man or woman at any time—*if they would just apply The Ultimate Secret Of Success.*

A Word About Heroes

As I finished the first edition of this book, the "O.J. Simpson trial" had sparked a national discussion of the relative wisdom or lack thereof of turning sports champions, entertainers, and other public celebrities into heroic role models. NBA star Charles Barkley publicly insisted "Athletes are not role models." Unfortunately, we cannot discourage countless young people from giving them hero status. The argument against viewing people as heroes based on their proclivity for making baskets, catching passes, packing concert halls, or delivering lines in movies is a good one, as too many seem to have an equal proclivity for squandering their status, money and time on drugs, alcohol, epic sexual misbehavior and violence.

Actually, there are plenty of REAL heroes all around us. While killing time at the airport, I got my shoes shined. The lady doing the job, I'd guess about 35 or 36 years old, was finishing her second shift of the day with me, at 6:00 PM. Just as she was finishing, the pay phone rang; as it turns out, her teenage daughter and son are required to call her every hour to check in. She is a divorced mother of two, a high school grad, with very limited marketable job skills, doing a relatively tough job, compensated by tips so the quality of her work, her attitude, her smile are critical; she is raising two teenagers; and she is saving up money to go back to school. I had to inquire and prod to find all this out. She was not complaining, not whining, not looking for pity. A real hero.

After a speaking engagement in Harrisburg, Pennsylvania, I was eating dinner in the Holiday Inn restaurant. Seated several tables away, alone, was a man about my age, in a wheelchair. His hands were apparently of little use to him. He dined on a bowl of soup and a soft drink, both consumed through a straw. When the check was brought to him, he somehow produced his wallet—I didn't see how—and extracted dollar bills from it with his teeth. Here was a man saddled with obvious shoulder-to-toes physical disabilities that made a simple journey to a restaurant difficult, tiring, possibly embarrassing. No one would criticize him for dropping out and copping out. But he refused to let his handicaps imprison him. A *real* hero.

During a weekend in Las Vegas. I was leaving Caesars Palace, the man getting his car from the valet ahead of me was also in a wheelchair. He and the valet knew each other and joked together as the man hoisted himself from his wheelchair into the car. The valet then left to retrieve my car. I walked over and asked the man if he would like help getting his wheelchair into his car. "Thanks," he said, "but it's not necessary. I've been doing this for myself for 30 years and I'm thankful that I can." One-handed, he folded up the wheelchair, pulled it into the car behind him, slid across the seat, and drove off. He, too, refused to be imprisoned by his handicap. A real hero.

I had reason to recall these two instances and individuals, when my Dad had a re-occurrence of an unusual neurological condition that put him flat on his back in the hospital, unable to sit up by himself, feed himself, stand, walk or do much of anything else. His doctors did their best to convince him that he, at best, might not go beyond being helped into a wheelchair. He set goals for regaining leg strength and balance. Then for control of the upper body. Then for feeding himself. Then for dressing himself. Then he moved from hospital to long-term care facility, today's euphemism for nursing home. Then he set goals for walking. For dressing himself. And finally he got into his own car and drove himself to his apartment. Then he came back to work at the office.

I once had a blind man in a sales organization I managed. He had not been blind at birth but had lost his sight in his late teens. He worked with his wife in our business, and was an enthusiastic, effective salesperson. He told me a favorite pastime was washing and waxing his car at ten or eleven o'clock at night, in the dark; it didn't matter to him but it sure bugged his neighbors! I asked him how it was that he had avoided bitterness or self-pity. He told me: "very early on, I got to meet and talk with many other blind people and I realized that many had let their lack of sight ruin their lives. They built little prisons for themselves and locked themselves in. I was determined not to do that." A real hero.

Each of these individuals' lives demonstrate that positive attitudes and actions, even in the most negative of circumstances, can make a big difference.

Who Else Is Afraid Of Public S-S-S-Speaking?

Phobias are real. I've had the privilege or working with Florence Henderson on a couple of TV projects, and gotten to know her—did you know that, following the cancellation of 'The Brady Bunch', her career dried up, and her fear of flying rose up and dominated her, crippling her pursuit of career opportunities, because she could not get on an airplane? Barbara Streisand stopped doing concerts thanks to uncontrollable stage freight. Johnny Carson reportedly suffered from incredible anxiety before every show. A comedian I know well, who I won't name, has such severe stage fright he vomits before most performances.

But there's not a phobia on earth that can't be treated, conquered, controlled.

Who's afraid of speaking in public? Just about everybody! Several surveys have shown that more people fear public speaking than fear heights, snakes, serious illness, accidental death or financial failure. One survey of Fortune 1000 executives revealed speaking to groups as their #1 fear. I've been fortunate to earn a large income from speaking; as my career progressed, from a few thousand dollars to $50,000.00 and up from each speech. But if you went back to the time in my childhood when I stuttered almost uncontrollably—when I could turn one short sentence into one long s-s-s-s-s-seminar—who would have predicted this career for me?

Although the problem lessened as I matured, to this day I am still "at risk" of getting "hung up" on a word, starting to stutter, embarrassing myself, on stage, on the phone or in conversation. Was it smart to choose careers in selling and speaking? Who would have blamed me for letting this influence my career choices? I refused to do that.

My friends John and Greg Rice were imprisoned by their midget size, until a man by the name of Glenn Turner ("Dare To Be Great") got a hold of them. John and Greg can't reach all the elevator buttons without something to stand on, and Glenn Turner was the first person to tell them that even "little men" could do big things. John and Greg have become very popular motivational speakers, on the subject of 'Thinking Big!'—even though they have to climb up onto a table so the audience can see them.

They achieved considerable success as real estate salesmen, even though they had to ask their customers to describe the things above sink level that they couldn't see. They've been featured on countless TV programs and in movies, built a sizable real estate investment business, and live a top quality lifestyle in sunny Florida.

For Every Handicap, Obstacle And Tragedy, There Are Two Stories.

Go ahead, name a handicap. Born and raised in a ghetto, as a latch-key kid, then surrounded by gangs, crime, drugs. A physical handicap. A crippling accident. A terrible disease. Illiteracy. Lack of education. A speech impediment. Severe phobia. Name the handicap. There are two stories to be found for every one you can think of. Story #1, unfortunately the most common, will be of people who've let that handicap imprison them. Story #2 will be of the person who has accomplished the most extraordinary things in spite of, in some cases because of, that very same handicap.

Each individual, by his or her actions, chooses which story will be theirs.

Imprisoning	The Action Model
I Can't	I Will
Resentment	Gratitude
Desire For Sympathy	Desire For Accomplishment
Dwelling On "It's Not Fair"	Search For Opportunities
Acceptance	Invention
"Maybe Tomorrow…"	Do It Now!
Withdrawal	Participation
Depression	Celebration Of Even Small Victories

∼

'IT'S AN IMPOSSIBLE SITUATION, BUT IT HAS POSSIBILITIES"

–Sam Goldwyn

Chapter 3 – Ben Glass

Ready, Set... Win!

Last month's message about how winners think about things, and then my reference to the college kids, drew some commentary and interest. As usual, I upset some people.

Sometimes it seems that no one wants to take personal responsibility for outcomes in life. Yes, where you are today is a direct result of the decisions you have made to date, good or bad. It's not about what life throws at you as much as it is about how you respond to life. Sure, bad things happen, but I can show you lots of highly successful people living lives of significance who have overcome HORRIBLE things that life threw at them.

The great news, and the promise of America, is that where you are today tells you nothing about where you'll end up—it only marks the **starting point**. There is abundant and unlimited opportunity for everyone. I've been talking to a lot of small business owners who have been complaining about the "recession."

I have to tell you that I am one who believes the foundations of the economy are sound—and—since I'm not running for office, no one will be putting me on a commercial trying to make fun of me for saying that.

I'm kind of tired of hearing people moan about the situation they find themselves in if they aren't doing anything to try to fix it. (An example might be GM—lost $38.7 billion in 2007, the same year that Toyota made $16 billion—same economy, right?) If we are gonna bail out GM, are we gonna bonus Toyota? If not, why not?

I'm tired of the media trying, night after night, to get it into everyone's heads that the sky is falling. Do you really feel sorry for all those people who bought houses they obviously could not afford just because "my real estate agent told me I *could* afford it" and some bank lent them the money? Should we really *suspend* foreclosures and let folks live in a house they can't afford—for free? Is the guy who's whining because it costs $125 to fill up his gas-guzzling SUV worthy of your sympathy? I doubt it.

Life isn't perfect, by any stretch, but here are my tips to stay out of Eeyore's storms:

1. **Never, ever stop learning.** I've got a stack of eight books (business, financial, motivational and biographical) sitting on my desk right now. I make a choice to read them instead of watching "America's Greatest Models" or some other silly TV show. Last I looked, the library was still free. In fact, I frequent a couple of

libraries, one near my office and one near my house… they are usually filled with people. Smart people.

2. **If you are running a business and it's not running so well, what are you doing to study your way out of the situation your choices got you into?** I promise that someone (and likely, many more than one) in your industry is kicking butt and taking names. Your job is to find out what they are doing that makes them successful.

3. **I get up no later than 5:30 every morning to make sure I have quiet time to plan my day and think about what I want to get accomplished.** I don't like to be in reaction mode all the time. Don't have enough time in your life? Try getting out of bed earlier. Not that hard.

4. **Associate with winners and dump the losers.** I deliberately seek out smart folks to hang out with and seek advice from. I've interviewed high school cross country runners and multi-millionaires to figure out what makes them tick. You'd be surprised at how much access you can get to really successful people if you are asking them *how they think* rather than begging them for money. If the people around you are *bringing you down,* exercise your choice to get new friends.

5. **I know where my priorities are—do you?** Really? If I looked over your shoulder and followed you around for a week, would I be able to *observe and identify* your highest priorities in life? Actions speak louder than words.

6. **I guard my time fiercely.** It's an irreplaceable asset. You and I have exactly the same amount of it. Some folks let others steal it from them. Do you?

This article first appeared in the October, 2008, edition of the BenGlassLaw newsletter.

Ben Glass has created a time management product based upon his own principles for "guarding" his time, available at MilitantTimeManagement.com.

Chapter 4 – Dan Kennedy

**Take Action To Take Charge Of
Every Aspect Of Your Life**

Once driving from Cincinnati, Ohio, to St. Louis, Missouri, to fight boredom, I was listening to a radio call-in show, hosted by a lady psychologist. I no longer remember her name or the name of the caller, but I certainly remember the conversation.

The caller, a woman, 40 years old, in her second marriage, spilled out a load of unhappiness and misery. Her husband didn't pay enough attention to her. Her kids were grown and no longer needed her. She was bored. Finally the host stopped her and said: "you will continue to be unhappy as long as you depend so much on others to make you happy."

I pulled the car off to the side of the road and jotted that down as a fill in the blank formula:

>   You Will Continue To Be Un-_____
>   As Long As You Depend On Others
>   To Make You _____

Then I wrote down a few examples:

**	You will continue to be unimportant
	as long as you depend on others to
	make you feel important.

**	You will continue to be un-prosperous
	as long as you depend on
	others to make you prosperous.

**	You will continue to be uninspired
	as long as you depend on
	others to make you inspired.

The Miracle Formula For Taking Charge Of Every Aspect Of Your Life

Let me tell you how this Miracle Formula came to me. The very first seminar I ever attended, now more than 35 years ago, where "success concepts" were presented was a real eye-opener for me. The speaker talked about what he called the most unpleasant success principle in the world. Well, who wants to hear about the most unpleasant anything? But I was there, so I listened. He said, repeatedly, "You are exactly where you really want to be."

Now let me tell you where I was. I had driven to the seminar in a 1960 Chevy Impala and it was not 1960. When it rained, this sad old car leaked from the top and from the bottom. The seats never dried out; they stayed musky damp in the summer, they froze and cracked in the winter. The car's frame was broken clear through, so its rear end was held up with a contraption of bailing wire, wood blocks and a turnbuckle. But there was no shame for this car. I'd paid just $25.00 for it, on payments, and it was all I could afford at the time. And the condition of the car was symbolic of a few other aspects of my life. So when that speaker said: you are exactly where you want to be—hey, I didn't like that very much.

It took me a while to stop arguing and start thinking.

Then I finally wrote down a "formula" from what I thought about, as a result of his statement. I could give it to you on the back of a matchbook—it doesn't require a whole BOOK to give you this—but don't let that diminish its importance. It is my non-humble opinion that this painfully arrived at formula has truly profound importance.

Here it is:

Control = Responsibility, Responsibility = Control

Everybody wants more control. If you take all your personal, career, financial and other goals, everything you think you want out of life, and boil all that down to a single overriding objective it is the desire for greater control. Greater control over finances, present and future. Greater control over your time and lifestyle. Greater control over your kids. Etc., Etc.

Ironically, as much as we desire greater control, we are the ones who give it all away. Every time we say…

- It's the location of our business

- It's the season

- It's the economy

- It's the supervisor who has it in for me

- It's the way I was brought up

- It's my partner/co-worker/spouse/etc.

- It's _____

Each and every time we say an "it's the…" We really DO two things simultaneously: one, we push away a small "weight" of responsibility, and that temporarily makes us feel better, but, two, we give up an equal-sized amount of control. Whenever we deny responsibility, we give up control. Get rid of a "pound" of responsibility, lose a pound's worth of control.

The Miracle Formula In Action: Why DOES One Person Prosper And Another Suffer?

I happen to know two people very well who are very much alike. They own two almost identical businesses. Their businesses are in neighboring, very similar towns. My observation is that they are equally skilled in the technical and administrative aspects of their business.

One, Peter E., has struggled for about seven years just to say in business. He has gained very little if any, financial ground during those years. His life is a day-to-day struggle for survival.

The other fellow, Robert L., started six years ago. His business has grown by 10% to as much as 30% each year, every year. He is now getting ready to turn it into a fortune through franchising.

When I talk with Peter E., I hear a lengthy discourse on all the outside influences that negatively affect his business. The economy, taxes, banks that won't give small business a fair shake, competition from huge corporations, and his list goes on and on and on. Every time I talk with Peter, I hear the same list. A broken record playing over and over again.

I acknowledge, by the way, that these factors do exist. I am frustrated by some of them myself. But the issue is not the existence of these factors. The issue is how much control Peter lets them have over his business. Every time Peter recites his list, he shuffles off responsibility for his situation, and that temporarily helps him feel better. But with the responsibility goes the control.

When I talk with Robert, these matters only occasionally come up. Instead, he talks excitedly about the innovative strategies he has discovered and developed to keep his business growing regardless of external influences. He exhibits healthy curiosity and quizzes me about strategies I've seen or discovered recently that might work for him. "How does that client of yours in x-business deal with this y-problem?" —he wants to know. Often, he'll say something like "I really screwed up on this situation. Let me tell you about the base I missed and what I'm doing about it."

Robert accepts all the responsibility for his success or failure, his errors and his achievements, and because he does, he retains control

Only 5% Exhibit Self-Reliant Behavior

Years ago, I did a speaking tour of all the CEO Clubs (Chief Executive Officers) in the country, for Joe Mancuso's Center For Entrepreneurial Management, and I talked with groups of corporate presidents in nearly a dozen different cities. If I heard it from one CEO, I heard it from a dozen: "It's getting harder and harder to find worthy people to promote from within."

"Why is that?" I asked.

"Only about 5% of all the people we employ consistently exhibit self-reliant behavior."

"What do you mean by 'self-reliant behavior'?"

One President answered this way: "Well, take the typists here in the office. They know that a proofreader checks their work for errors, so they rely on her rather than bothering to check their own work and consistently present her with typing done right the first time. Then we've got fifty sales reps in the field, Accounting has to constantly chase and nag every one of them to get their paperwork. My Sales Manager told me the other day that we've got one guy who we give wake-up calls to."

Another President said, "We have about 20 people in the Chicago plant. Only three or four consistently get here on time, ready to work. I figure about 5% of all the people we've ever employed, in all the different jobs, accept full responsibility for successful completion of every aspect of their jobs."

The word "typist" dates this a bit, doesn't it? Sorry to say, this entire situation hasn't improved in the years elapsed since I first wrote this. It has gotten worse. SLOPPINESS is epidemic, from the simplest on-the-job tasks, like putting the correct items in the bag handed through the drive-in window if you're a fast food worker or knowing how to get to a booked destination if a limo driver to the more critical, like staying awake if you're an air traffic controller or delivering the right dosage if you're a nurse in a hospital. The #1 reason business owners fire and replace vendors, suppliers and professionals is this kind of sloppiness. The #1 complaint I hear today from employers about those they weed out is this sloppiness. It is important to understand that all this sloppiness represents irresponsibility. Evidence that the person is not to be trusted.

When you think through what these CEO's said, you have a simple answer to a long list of questions...

- How can I move ahead in my career?

- How can I get a better job?

- How can I start my own business?

- How can I have a better relationship?

- How can I maintain a positive outlook?

- How can I make more money?

Most people have unsaid extensions to these kinds of questions:

- How can I move ahead in my career – *when others have more education than I do?... when the boss likes Steve better than me?*

- How can I get a better job – *when the economy's so bad?*

- How can I start my own business – *when I haven't got any money?*

… and so on.

The answer to these questions and many more like them is: self-reliant behavior.

How Long Will You Wait Before Taking Charge?

The many times that that I followed General Schwartzkopf on a program, I listened as he posed this rhetorical question: *if you are put in charge, when you are put in charge, what should you do? TAKE CHARGE!*

He was talking about the very essence of leadership—not waiting, not procrastinating, not looking around to copy how others did it or are doing it, not waiting for a committee to cover your butt with its recommendations; instead, stepping forward to do what needs to be done and to do what is right.

All too often, even when an individual finally gets the chance to be "in charge" that he has coveted, he accomplishes little. For years, other players on the NBA Chicago Bulls grumbled and groused about being stuck in the shadow of Michael Jordan. They coveted the chance to command that spotlight and lead the team. But when Michael Jordan retired, that spotlight searched vainly for that team's next leader. In 1994, it couldn't find one. The most logical heir-apparent embarrassed himself and his entire team in the playoffs by throwing a 'hissy fit' over not being named by the coach as the man to get the ball and try the final shot in the final seconds of a closely contested play-off game. This would-be leader let his ego control his actions. Incredibly, he refused to go back in from the time out and give his best efforts to the play that had been called. You can look around and see such individuals' squandering their opportunities constantly in just this way.

But I would go even farther: *why wait until you are put in charge?* Take charge anyway. The fact is: there's a leadership vacuum just about everywhere. Maybe in your home. Probably in your business or place of employment. In your industry, in your community, in your church, in your country. And I suggest this leadership vacuum offers you the opportunity you seek to change your life for the better. Let me give you a very down-to-earth example:

Mary S. was at a seminar I presented for doctors some years ago. She was there with her husband, a dentist. She pulled me aside on a break. "Could I talk to you alone for a minute?" So she and I ducked out of the meeting room, went down the hall, and found an empty meeting room to step into.

"I'm so frustrated," she told me. "There are so many things you've been talking about that we could do to build up the practice. We keep going to seminars, hearing good ideas, but my husband never gets anything new implemented. Nothing happens. The staff now knows that when he comes back from a seminar talking about new ideas, all they have to do is wait a few days and it'll all blow over. And the practice hasn't grown a bit in three years."

"What kind of things would you have him do?" I asked.

"Join the Chamber of Commerce, attend meetings and make contacts with other business people in the community," she said. "And start a mailing campaign to area business owners and executives. And put out a monthly newsletter for our past and present patients. And put together a little how-to book, something like *'How To Keep Healthy Teeth For Life.'* And, in the office, our reception area desperately needs re-decorated. The staff needs some help with handling telephone calls, especially from new patients calling in because of our yellow pages ad. And—"

"Wait a minute," I raised my hand like a traffic cop and brought her to a halt. "Mary, these all sound like inarguably good ideas to me."

"But he won't do any of them," she said sadly.

"Well, Mary," I asked, "What are you waiting for?"

For the first time that night, Mary was speechless. She returned to the meeting room with a particularly thoughtful look on her face.

You see, it's one thing to complain about another person's failure to pick up the ball and run with it. In this case, Mary was certainly justified in being frustrated with her husband's lack of ambition and initiative. But she'd been complaining to him and about him for three years. She'd been frustrated for three years. Obviously, that wasn't going to change anything. Her only apparent options: accept him and things exactly as-is and stop being aggravated, continue being frustrated every day of her life for the rest of her life, divorce him and leave, or pick up the ball and do some running of her own.

Most would choose one of the first two options. Thoreau observed "Most men (and women) lead lives of quiet desperation."

About a year later, Mary S. appeared at another of my many seminars for doctors. Again she cornered me on a break, apart from her husband. "I want to tell you," she began, "that I was very angry with you and the way you answered me that night. I wanted some sympathy. And I wanted you to go have a tough talk with my husband. But I sure didn't want you to challenge *me*."

"Should I apologize?" I asked.

"Hardly," she answered. "Let me tell you about my new life." Mary no longer worked in the office as a dental assistant. Instead she had hired her replacement, then appointed herself 'Director Of Marketing.' She joined the Chamber of

Commerce, a businesswomen's club, a Toastmasters group, and enrolled in a Dale Carnegie class. She assembled a book—*"Secrets Of A Healthy Smile For Life"*—and she began speaking to groups of school children, PTA meetings, civic groups, everywhere she could on behalf of the practice. She put together a practice newsletter, assigned writing tasks to other staff members and occasionally even to patients, got it done, published and out every month. She designed a new 'Family Plan' to promote to the practice's patients. She created and promoted 'Patient Appreciation Weeks.'

In five months, the practice doubled. Although shocked at first, her husband adapted to her new role and new interests. And he was kept pretty busy just handling the new patient flow anyway.

"Now I work just three or four hours a day, doing all the marketing and promotion for the practice—I'm our 'Mrs. Outside', he's our 'Mr. Inside', and I've even got time for my new venture, creating and publishing health-related coloring books for kids, distributed through dentists nationwide. *I'm not waiting anymore,*" she concluded.

Now, what are you waiting for?

"Are you pleased with your present place in the world? If your answer is yes, what's your next port of call? If your answer is no, what are you going to do about it?

–Earl Nightingale
From: *Earl Nightingale's Greatest Discovery*
Published by Dodd/Mead

Chapter 5 – Ben Glass

Thriving In Times Of Crisis

Hans Beck died in February. Who, you say? Hans Beck, inventor of Playmobil Toys. You know…those three-inch pirates, cowboys and knights. The ones that have no knees!! My Kevin loves them! Some have been in my house for almost 25 years! Extraordinarily popular, durable toys. Simple toys.

Hans Beck was a millionaire. Over 2 billion of these Playmobil toy figures have been sold. Do you know when they first became a viable product? During a severe economic crisis. In the early 1970's there was a global oil crisis. Since toys are made of plastic and plastic comes from oil, the crisis threatened the toy industry.

While Hans Beck could have, I imagine, simply read the headlines of the day and given up, he didn't allow the media or the government to control the outcome of his life. He didn't just wait to be run over by an economic catastrophe. He reinvented. He had to design something that kids still liked, but which was smaller. The toys had no knees, no noses but a stylized design.

According to the Washington Post obituary, his new toys were a smashing success, selling more than a million dollars' worth in the first year.

Yes, we are in an economic crisis now, but I know plenty of individuals and small businesses who are thriving. One told me that he wouldn't notice that there was a recession going on unless he read the newspapers (which he avoids doing because rarely is there anything actually useful in today's newspapers—and they wonder why they are all dying).

What do these successful people have in common? First, they aren't sitting on their butts waiting for a "bailout." In fact, they resent this whole "bailout" idea as un-American. (Do you know how many cars GM would have to sell to repay $16 billion dollars? Has America really missed the failed car companies that the market killed off? But… I digress.)

Second, they are learners. They recognize that what human beings have that animals don't is the God-given ability to learn new things and then use their consciousnesses to take what they have learned and make it bigger and better. The world is waiting for the next great idea.

Third, they hate hanging out with "Eeyore." You know Eeyore. The world is always gloomy, the sky is falling and we have no control over our impending doom. If they have friends who are "Eeyores," they dump them (harsh, I know…but you have a choice. I've dumped plenty of Eeyores from my life). They get out of groups that are filled with Eeyores.

Fourth, they seek out and find other winners and then they associate with them. They are out there, folks.

This article first appeared in the March, 2009 edition of the BenGlassLaw newsletter.

Chapter 6 – Dan Kennedy

Take Action To Get The Know-How You Need

Not knowing how to do something has never stopped me from setting out to do it, and I've become convinced that anybody can become competent, even expert at just about anything; there are books, courses, classes, teachers, mentors, coaches, newsletters, associations, an absolute abundance of information linked to virtually any and every skill or ability or occupation you can think of. A whole lot of it is readily available, free. More at very modest cost. Some, pricey.

The internet has made it ridiculously easy to obtain information, education and training. The trek to the library replaced by a button, by typing in a search term. Almost every provider of training offers a lot of it free at their web sites as outreach for new customers, just as we do at www.NoBSBooks.com and www.DanKennedy.com, and at www.Pete-The-Printer.com. YouTube is full of video presentations on every imaginable subject by authors, experts, speakers. Any industry and most competitors and many prospective clients or customers can be thoroughly researched without leaving your easy chair via the web. Yet, with all this easy access, I find people getting lazier and lazier about doing any homework at all. Professionals who go to some trouble and exert effort to get a meeting with me, to attempt to sell me their services, have not even bothered to Google® me before the appointment. New clients who meet with me often lack even the most basic statistical information about their target market readily, easily available to them at their own trade association's web site. People with problems they seek advice for have not even bothered to investigate what information is available.

Please hear this: absence of intellectual curiosity about both the specific business or other pursuit you are engaged in, about success in general, and even about the world around you produces the same basic result as if you had the I.Q. of a tree frog. Further, failure to act on intellectual curiosity in a constant way is simple evidence of lack of true ambition. I am fond of telling of being backstage with Donald Trump at an event where we were both speakers and, after brief conversation, being asked by The Donald: what three books are you reading now? There's much to be learned by the question. And there's another lesson in the end of the story I usually don't tell because of time. He scribbled down one of the titles I mentioned, handed the paper scrap to an assistant hovering behind him, and said, "Get me this book."

Most people stop far, far, far short of aggressive, ambitious intellectual curiosity—they don't even demonstrate any initiative or self-reliance when it comes to their own work, their own business and the specific know-how needed for it. I am frequently amazed and dismayed at the people who seek me out and ask questions that evidence they haven't even done an ounce of homework or research on their own. A business owner came to me after I finished delivering a speech on advertising and marketing, handed me the advertising flyer he'd prepared and invested his hard-earned money in having printed and distributed, and said, "What do you think?"

I had a few questions of my own. "Before you put this together," I said, "what books did you go and get about writing advertising headlines? About advertising in general?" And I could have asked a dozen more questions along these same lines. The answers, were, frankly, pitiful. Non-existent. He had done nothing, nada, zero to prepare himself for the task of putting together effective advertising flyers. When you look at this objectively, from the outside in, it's pretty obvious that this is stupid behavior. And quite bluntly, if you insist on behaving stupidly, you do not deserve positive results.

Ignorance about any particular subject is forgivable and, fortunately, fixable. Stupidity is another story altogether.

The Serious Student At Work

When I became earnest about using more humor in my speeches and seminars, and getting good at using it, for example, I found no shortage of assistance out there. Beyond simply observing and analyzing great humorists and comedians, I found plenty of books on the subject, Esar's *Comic Encyclopedia*, videos, seminars, newsletters, and home study courses. I learned "timing" from listening to a fantastic humorous speaker, Dr. Charles Jarvis, from comedian Shelley

Berman, and others, over and over and over again. I read all the classic masters – Benchley, Thurber, I read all the contemporary humorists, I read everything Steve Allen ever wrote, I found 'old' comedy records, I subscribed to humor services like Orbens. I became a very serious student of humor. Gradually I transitioned from picking and telling jokes to creating original material, from jokes to humorous stories. I did a whole lot of homework. I became accomplished enough at it to make a great deal of money as a professional speaker and, as writer, consultant and coach, help a lot of other speakers improve their efficacy. I even wrote a book about use of humor in selling, as speaker or writer: *Make 'Em Laugh And Take Their Money.*

When I got involved in teaching advertising, marketing and sales to doctors of chiropractic, I became a serious student of the chiropractic profession. I subscribed to the profession's journals, I got and read books, I visited offices, I went to seminars, I asked questions of doctors. In a few months, I knew enough and sounded so much like a chiropractor, that we had to continually correct doctors who called me "Dr. Kennedy" and convinced themselves I was one of them. To this day, I'll be walking through a hotel lobby, airport, mall and have a chiropractor yell out, "hello Dr. Kennedy!" And, although I would never give an adjustment, I can do a decent exam, a good report of findings, I can sell people on chiropractic better than most chiropractors, and I could operate a practice. I could go to a convention and easily pass myself off as a doctor if I chose to. I'll bet I could go to an office and get myself hired as an associate doctor.

Some years back, I worked closely with a client in the retail theft control business. His company dealt with employee and delivery man theft in supermarkets, convenience stores and drug stores (where it is an immense problem). Then, I subscribed to all the trade journals of the supermarket, convenience store and drug store industry, and assembled articles about theft from several years of back issues. I read what books I could find on the subject. I studied my client's materials. I learned the language of retail finance. To this day, I can walk into any such store or restaurant and, in 5 minutes, tell you whether or not the employees are stealing and, if so, show you the "hidden evidence" that proves it. And I could give a seminar to retailers on the subject and no one would question my status as an expert.

I'm not bragging. I'm just pointing out that it isn't very difficult to quickly acquire expertise in a given area, if that's what you want to do. But it's amazing to me the number of people who just never bother.

When I worked with the chiropractors, I used to ask groups for a show of hands – how many had really studied even one book or course on how to sell. In most groups, less than half; yet everyday, their incomes depend on their effectiveness at selling… selling the public and new prospective patients on chiropractic, selling new patients their recommendations and their fees. They're not alone. Just about every business or occupation is a composite of several different types of expertise, but most people master one and are content being an amateur in the others.

If not knowing about something stands between you and what you want to accomplish, get busy and go get that know-how. If really is that simple.

The 7 Ways To Get Smarter About Virtually any Subject – FAST

1.   **Find and read at least a year's back issues of the related trade or specialty magazines.**

Every business, industry, occupation, vocation, hobby or special interest—from cooking to computer programming, from ostrich farming to searching for lost gold mines, from long-haul truck driving to golfing, from writing to woodworking, from Astrology to zoology—has one, in most cases, several magazines all its own. In these magazines, the experts write articles, are interviewed and profiled, how-to secrets are revealed, advertisers promote their wares.

2.   **Answer a lot of the ads you find in these magazines.**

Let all those advertisers try to sell you their products and services. Soon, you'll be deluged with information. All coming to you, free.

3. **Find the top experts, most successful people and most celebrated people in the field.**

Such people have probably written books, recorded audio programs, they may sell such products, seminars, consulting, coaching and/or they may even be approachable just to talk with or visit with free. Seek out the best and the brightest and find out how you can best turn their experience into your knowledge. Surprisingly, even in competitive fields, these outspoken experts and super achievers exist.

Some years back, I worked with a chiropractor who started his own practice immediately after school. Almost immediately. First, armed with a list he had painstakingly compiled of 50 of the most successful, most respected chiropractors in the country, he got in his car and drove across country, north, south, east and west, going to each of their offices, asking if he could observe, take the doctor to lunch or dinner and pick his brain, visit with the staff, and so on. Forty-nine of the fifty were gracious, generous, encouraging and helpful. He arrived home with what he called 'A Master Practice-Building Plan From The Masters Of The Profession'. He had great confidence in this plan. He implemented it with natural enthusiasm and positive expectation. And he built a record-breaking practice in short order.

If I were to start in a brand new business today, I would follow his example.

4. **Find the books written by "the OLD masters."**

Just about every field has "old masters", whose works are hard to find or even out of print, who many ignore as passed by time and no longer important. They're wrong.

In the selling field, every salesperson should read books by Frank Bettger, Red Motley, Robert Trailins, to name a few, from the 1950's, the 1940's, and earlier if you can find them. Robert Trailins' "old book", *Dynamic Selling*, published by Prentice-Hall a long time ago, to be found only in libraries or used bookstores, offers better advice on crafting powerful appointment-getting presentations than any book, seminar or course I'm aware of.

In direct-response advertising and copywriting, today's top pros, like my friends Gary Halbert and Ted Nicholas, and I, constantly refer novices to the works of the "old masters," Robert Collier, Claude Hopkins, Victor Schwab and others, dating back to the 1930's.

I would add, of course, the suggestion that you read MY books, and I'm reluctant to say it, but I'm reaching the "old master" status. For selling, read my *No B.S. Sales Success* book. For marketing, read *No B.S. Direct Marketing For Non-Direct Marketing Businesses,* as well as *The Ultimate Marketing Plan* and *The Ultimate Sales Letter.* For entrepreneurship, read *No B.S. Business Success* and *No B.S. Wealth Attraction For Entrepreneurs.* They're all readily available at bookstores,

BN.com, amazon.com, or you can get free information about them at www.NoBSBooks.com.

5. **Join trade associations or clubs.**

The "learning curve shortcuts" available through trade association membership and attending association conventions and workshops is remarkable. The opportunity to make dozens and dozens of important and beneficial contacts is even greater.

Most associations have archives of audio recordings from past years' conventions and workshops, so you can "attend" two, five, even ten years of past events as if a time machine was at your disposal.

Many national associations have state, regional or city "chapters", with easily accessible meetings and seminars, usually all at very modest costs.

At Glazer-Kennedy Insider's Circle™, we now have local chapters and coaching groups, and you can find information about them at dankennedy.com. If you received this book from a business expert in a particular field, he may offer options for coaching and mastermind groups to join as well.

Why Do Top Performers Use Coaches?

When the legendary golfer Arnold Palmer needed to tune-up his game, to compensate for his age, he sought out a young-by-comparison, 26 year old 'swing coach'. This should not surprise. It's widely known that virtually all top athletes in every sport rely on coaches. But why do top sales professionals, small business owners, professionals in private practice, entrepreneurs, authors, speakers and executives need coaches too?

Having *personally* had over 400 high-flying entrepreneurs and self-employed professionals in my own coaching programs, assisted with coaching programs and groups reaching thousands in fields like chiropractic, dentistry and financial services, and been a leader and innovator in the development of business coaching thus essentially spawning hundreds of niche-industry coaches, in aggregate coaching nearly 1-million people, I think I have a pretty good understanding of why coaching seems to work so well for so many top-performers in business. There are six reasons:

1. Being Questioned and Challenged

2. Being Held Accountable

3. Being Listened To

4. Being Accepted

5. Being Motivated

6. Being Recognized For Achievements

Different people have different needs at different times in their lives and different stages of development in their businesses, but everyone can benefit from some at any and every time.

Questioned And Challenged

The more successful you are, the less likely the people who work for you or are around you all the time are going to be to challenge your ideas. It's easy to wind up surrounded by "yes men"—and to like it! The outside coach with no axe to grind can be both objective and frank. Most importantly, he can ask the provocative questions that force you to defend and, at times, re-evaluate your ideas.

Held Accountable

On many occasions, as a speaker, I have been backstage in "green room" conversations with legendary athletes like NFL quarterbacks Joe Montana and Troy Aikman, Olympian Mary Lou Retton, boxer-turned-super entrepreneur George Foreman, coaches like Tom Landry,

Jimmy Johnson, Lou Holtz. The athletes all agreed that top performers personally hold themselves accountable to gruelingly high standards, but still, were it not for accountability to teammates, fans and coaches, and being held accountable by coaches who monitor their statistics, show them film and critique it, and work with them for improvement, they would never have reached the levels of success they did. Every coach agrees that the very act of reporting to someone and being held accountable by someone automatically improves performance. A business/life coach can ably fulfill this need.

Listened To

A *Newsweek Magazine* article about professional business and life coaches described us as "part therapist – part consultant." That's fair. A lot of entrepreneurs, executives and sales pros have no one to talk to about business OR personal matters who they dare "let their hair down" with… who will listen without agenda of self-interest or judgment… who can serve as sounding board. I find, often, that a client will talk his way to his own terrific answer, solution or plan of action if I'll just listen. Having to discuss your business, goals, problems, ideas and questions with a knowledgeable coach who listens forces you to stop, think, focus and organize your own thoughts and sometimes acquire or assemble information—all valuable action that otherwise may take a perpetual back-seat to day-to-day activity. A great coaching question originally posed by author Joe Karbo is: "are you too busy making a living to make any real money?" A coach can forcibly slow you down, get you off the hamster wheel you're running on, and insist that you think through your intentions and actions out loud. In group coaching environments, a famous strategist Jay Abraham and I call this "hot-seating"; putting you on the hot seat, in front of the group, thinking out loud and being aided or questioned as you go, everybody working without a net.

Accepted

I call myself and my most successful clients "RENEGADE Millionaires"—but we are seen by most around us as misfits, loose cannons, difficult and unreasonable people, and aggravations! Because we Renegade Millionaires violate most industry norms, reject traditions and limits, aggressively and determinedly push forward our ideas, and because, candidly, we are both exceptionally effective and surprisingly dysfunctional in one way or another, we think, talk and act very differently from almost everyone around us in daily life. A lot of successful entrepreneurs suffer isolation and loneliness, feel like "fish out of water", even have trouble explaining themselves and what they do to "civilians". Being part of a mastermind group comprised of like-minded renegades, organized, facilitated and coached by a capable leader, is invigorating.

One of the core human needs is to be accepted for who you are, without need of mask or cautious editing of expressed thought, and a relationship with the right coach provides that.

Motivated

Surely a top pro athlete paid millions of dollars to play a game doesn't need "motivated", right? Actually, the fact that they are paid millions of dollars, often win, lose or draw, means they do need a great deal of other motivation. In almost every locker room, grown men paid millions are awarded game balls and trophies. Coaches cry, hug, atta-boy! Ultimately, all motivation is self-motivation, but it is fueled by the people and ideas you associate with, the successes of others you're exposed to, the encouragement you get. Paul J. Meyer, one of 'the grand old men' of the success philosophy field and founder of Success Motivation Institute gave a speech titled *"Who Motivates The Motivator?"*, pointing out that leaders must accept personal responsibility for their own motivation, but that everybody needs motivational influencing.

Recognized For Achievements

Everybody thrives on recognition and celebration – but to whom can the entrepreneur brag? Certainly not his employees, competitors or vendors. Hard to be welcomed home as a conquering hero. A good coach, singly, or in concert with a mastermind group, who understands and genuinely appreciates your accomplishments fills an important gap in entrepreneurial life.

What Exactly Is Business/Life Coaching?

Coaching is delivered many different ways: one-to-one, in person, by phone or online; one-to-group, in mastermind meetings and workshops and field trips, via teleseminars, webinars, and peer-to-peer online resources; and combinations and hybrids thereof. It sometimes has as pre-requisite study of certain courses or resources, attendance at certain seminars, or the meeting of certain income or other qualifications. It is priced by the hour or day, by the month, by the year, or fee for program. Sometimes, coaches' programs also include support services and/or done-for-them tools and resources to use in your business. Some coaching programs or groups are strictly limited in size while others are open, some feature territorial exclusivity or competitor lock-out, most do not. Ethical coaches do two primary things: one, structure their relationship with and deliverables for clients to be as valuable and effective as possible *for those who implement them,* and two, exert best efforts to select clients they genuinely believe will benefit and profit from their coaching. It has to be said that buying coaching is not a substitute for implementation!

Chapter 7 – Ben Glass

Lessons From An Iranian Refugee

Don't Sit Back and Wait for Opportunities to Come Your Way

In an economy that has many recent graduates and even seasoned professionals waiting for job opportunities to come their way, a story of a 37-year-old man from Iran shows that success is still possible, you just have to go out and find it.

Payam "Peter" Tabibian, who was profiled in the Washington Post, is not afraid of hard work or taking entry-level jobs to learn about a business. Tabibian and his family fled Iran in 1982 and eventually came to the United States. From an early age, Tabibian looked for opportunities to make money and has had many successful ventures.

Below are some lessons that can be learned from Tabibian.

Be Willing to Learn from Top to Bottom

When Tabibian was a 14-year-old boy, he took a job at Burger King, which included the unglamorous tasks of taking out the trash, washing dishes and cleaning the parking lot. Some students may have turned up their noses at the idea of performing these job duties, but in Tabibian's own words, "I was curious. I learned everything. It was great." This entry-level job helped prepare Tabibian for a future lucrative career.

Don't Be Afraid to Work Hard

Tabibian worked at numerous Burger Kings and eventually became a restaurant manager at the age of 17, which made him the youngest manager ever at the L'Enfant Plaza restaurant. His schedule was hectic, as he attended high school in the morning, then went to work in the afternoon. He also worked at a grocery store with a shift that started at midnight.

Have the Discipline to Save Money

Many people spend what they make and put aside little in savings, but not Tabibian. He saved a lot of what he made and was able to stockpile more than $30,000 as a young person. Tabibian was able to use his savings to invest in additional businesses, including vending machines that brought in up to $10,000 in just one month.

Search Out Opportunities

Tabibian's business ventures have ranged from selling neckties to gumballs, but there is one central theme—he searches out opportunities and doesn't sit back and wait for them to come his way.

In April 2008, Tabibian and a partner used $500,000 of their own money to launch a fast food restaurant called Z-Burger.

Although the industry is crowded, Tabibian has been able to find a way to differentiate his restaurant from the others and his Tenleytown store now grosses about $2.8 million a year and has a net profit of nearly $700,000. Tabibian only takes out a $60,000 salary and puts the rest back into the business. He plans to open additional stores.

According to Tabibian, "in two or three years, I am going to be a different man. I am going to be one of the richest men in this town." Based on his track record, this possibility is very real. Tabibian knows what it takes to be successful and there are many valuable lessons that can be learned from his story.

Yes, things are tougher now than they were three years ago, especially for high school and college graduates, but let me ask you this: If you are young and having a hard time in this economy, what are you doing to let others know that you are SERIOUS about creating opportunity for yourself? I just looked at some alarming statistics about the number of people who subscribe to and read People magazine and the number of people who subscribe to and read Success magazine. What are *you* reading?

This article first appeared in the January, 2010, edition of the BenGlassLaw newsletter.

Chapter 8 – Dan Kennedy

Take Action To Shed Excess Baggage And Discover New Capabilities

In a novel *"Line Of Duty"*, author Michael Grant has one of his characters deliver this: *"A guy I fish with once told me a funny story. He'd just bought an anchor, and as he went forward to tie it to the anchor line, he slipped and fell overboard. Suddenly, he's sitting on the bottom of the lake in fifteen feet of water, cradling his brand new anchor. He didn't want to let go, but he was running out of breath. Realizing his choice was drowning or losing the anchor, he reluctantly let go and swam to the surface."* The character in the novel, a police detective, went on to say: *"The Job has been my anchor and I've been holding on to it for 23 years. I don't want to let go either, but I've run out of breath."*

Most people can be caught holding onto prized anchors.

Another way to look at it is in terms of roles. A person gets so used to a role, so comfortable in that role that, even though unhappy, the fear and trauma of stepping outside the role feels worse than the pain of continuing in it. Such roles include: The Victim *(why me—it's so unfair)*, The Martyr *(I gave up everything for you)*, The Last Angry Man *(I'm mad as hell at everybody and everything – but I will keep taking it),* The Misunderstood Genius, and so on.

So much of our current thoughts and actions have their basis in childhood. My aversion to having a large house with a yard to care for is the direct result of growing up in over-large homes where there was always some damned thing in need of repair or cleaning or replacement, some project to be done or, worse, some disaster to be battled – like, in our second house, a basement that flooded every spring to such a degree that the neighborhood's animals lined up two by two outside. And growing up with yards always in need of mowing or weeding (until I discovered that a hungry Shetland pony on a tether made lawn mowers obsolete). Anyway, I am emotionally averse to all that. Of course, that's obvious. No need for years of therapy to figure that out. And it's not particularly important. But it is only one of who knows how many examples of today's thoughts, attitudes, likes, dislikes, fears, ideas and behaviors firmly rooted in childhood programming that has never been challenged or even re-considered.

In cases where this does no harm, or even helps, I suppose there's no need to tinker with it. But what about the baggage that does burden, the anchor that does drown, the past programming that does limit? It is plain as can be that people are controlled—yes, controlled—throughout their adult lives by limits that were set and by behaviors that were prescribed early on, then never challenged.

If you are not achieving the results you tell yourself you want out of life, it may very well be that these set-in-the-past restrictions are getting in your way. In the late 1980's, I had the privilege of editing and assembling a new audio program featuring the recorded radio broadcasts and lectures of Dr. Maxwell Maltz, famous in the 1950's for his best-selling book, *'Psycho-Cybernetics'*, in which he advanced the idea that everything from a person's financial success to the accuracy of his golf swing was controlled by a subconsciously held, very detailed "self-image", largely constructed out of childhood programming and experiences, then reinforced through self-talk. Dr. Maltz was first pointed in this direction while in practice as a cosmetic surgeon; many patients came believing that getting some physical flaw fixed—a nose bobbed, breasts enlarged—would alter the way they felt about themselves and make them happier but even after surgery that made them beautiful or handsome on the outside, they still thought, talked and acted as if nothing had changed. From this observation, Dr. Maltz made the giant leap—now virtually accepted as universal truth – that a person can practice the perfect golf swing, for example, all he wants and still suffer an awesome slice, unless and until he somehow alters the image he has of himself as a golfer.

There is a kind of mental magnetism connected to the self-image. Earl Nightingale put it this way: *we become what we think about most.* Of course, that's not instantly, literally true; if it were, as a teenager I'd have become Playmate Of The

Month. But, over time, it is true. People do think themselves sick. Or old before their time. Or a victim. A perpetual loser.

Certainly, experience alters the self-image. For years, a person considers himself hopelessly clumsy. Then, out of dire necessity, he picks up tools and fixes something and is shocked to discover the awkward lack of coordination of teenage years has been replaced by reasonable facility, and he can drive a nail, and now has to question the long-held, limiting self-image: *hey, wait a minute, maybe I'm not so clumsy after all.*

There's no reason that has to happen only by happy accident. Instead, you can benefit enormously by testing your limits. *"Let's just see if this is still true."* The more of this you do, the more likely you are to uncover abilities you didn't know you had.

In *"The Hobbit"* Bilbo Baggins said, "I don't like adventures. They make one late for dinner." That is the attitude of far too many people. At age 25, David Smith – college drop-out, gambler, playboy, occasional saloonkeeper, began what he has called a 'healing journey' of exploration. By the time he was 35, he had become the first person to swim from Africa to Europe, had kayaked 2,000 miles down the Nile, run a marathon with tribesmen in Kenya, and put himself through a number of other incredible adventures. (You can read about his story in his book *"Healing Journey: The Odyssey Of An Uncommon Athlete"*, published by Sierra Club Books.) David inscribed the book to me, "to a man who knows the art of adventure." Frankly, I wish that was a bit truer than it actually is. But I do stretch. I do test. Constantly. Why not? Fortunately I grew up hearing "how do you know until you try?" You don't.

Take A Closer Look At The Labels Sewn On You

Labels get sewn on children—then they often stay on them as they become adults, even though they are no longer correct (if they ever were). Consider these labels:

- Such a CLUMSY AND AWKWARD CHILD

- SLOW LEARNER

- BOOKWORM

- SHY WALLFLOWER…THE QUIET TYPE

- DAYDREAMER

- Just not good with _____
  (math; spelling; sports, etc.)

Or consider these: Clint Eastwood was told by an executive at Universal Pictures that he "had no future as an actor" because he had a chipped tooth, an Adams apple that was too prominent, and talked too slow. Best-selling, millionaire author Scott Turow (*"Presumed Innocent"*) must be a shock to his high school English teacher; Scott got an "F" in that course.

In his first fight, Joe Louis was knocked down six times in three rounds, and labeled by one sportswriter as a "doormat with no future." Charles Schultz, creator of *"Peanuts"*, was turned down for a job as a cartoonist at the Disney Studios, and told he "lacked talent".

What Life's Winners Do About Their Labels: The Artichoke Factor

The labels of football teams are interesting. In many cases, there are images invoked for the players to live up to. The Los Angeles Raiders, for example, with the pirate logo, silver and black colors, "Raiders" name, all that calls for a very tough, aggressive, physical style of play. Players have talked about there being something "special" about that tradition; they've said that when you put on a Raiders uniform, something happens to you inside. For years, the Pittsburgh Steelers were famous for their "Steel Curtain Defense." For obvious reasons, you'll probably never see a football team named "The Williamsburg Librarians."

Which brings us to the small Scottsdale Community College, in 1975, with a very liberal student body opposed to competitive sports. They considered football frivolous, superficial and representative of a too-violent, too-male-dominated society. As a symbol of their feelings, they elected the artichoke as the official mascot of the college's football team. Imagine the ridicule you'd suffer suiting up and taking the field as a player on The Scottsdale Artichokes!

The Artichokes played their games at a local high school, because their own practice field had no bleachers, and no funds were ever approved for any. Their head coach, John Aviantos, had no scholarships to offer in recruiting talented players. Burdened with the artichoke name, given no recruiting tools, minimal funds, Coach Aviantos still won four conference championships, went to two bowl games, and never had a losing season. Coach Aviantos coined the term "The Artichoke Factor" to represent the aspect of a person's character that inspires him to rise to a challenge, to look at the labels that have been sewn on, disagree, and tear them off. **"Successful people rarely start out labeled as most-likely-to-succeed,"** Coach told me. In the sixth year of his tenure there, an 8-foot-high sculpture of an artichoke was erected—a monument to Aviantos' determination not to let a negative, humiliating label stay sewn on his football program and his players.

Labels Sewn On "Accidentally" In Childhood Are One Thing – Labels Attached To Us As Adults Are Another

The CBS news anchor Dan Rather once commented that one of the most shocking lessons in life is the discovery that not everyone wishes you well. There is a surprising amount of jealousy, envy and resentment directed at high achievers in every field. The more you try to do and the more you do, the more you will be subject to it.

The "Idiot" label has been hastily sewn on many people by a critical media, including President Ronald Reagan, Vice-President Dan Quayle, and more recently, Governor Sarah Palin. Every time this is done, considerable accomplishment that contradicts the label is ignored—why let facts get in the way? Tom Monaghan, the original founder and developer of Domino's Pizza, once commented about how easily and quickly he went from being "boy genius" to "village idiot". Once, while engaged in a complex consulting project for a large, troubled corporation—for which I was being paid a million dollars—I asked for the list of their franchisees to review and choose some to personally interview. The list I was given included a former CEO of the company, long retired, who had a single store in a small town to, as they put it, piddle around with. The current corporate leaders made it clear they thought this guy of no current relevance—basically, an idiot. I found him to be far saner than the present management team, and afterward, suggested they cancel my contract and hire him to right the ship.

Most of the severest, most persistent, most sarcastic and mocking critics of Reagan, Quayle, Palin have never been asked by either political party to run as President or Vice-President, never campaigned for and won a Senate seat or state Governor's office or served in the White House. The vast majority of critics are people of little accomplishment. There has only been one movie critic in history to ever write and produce a movie—and it was a terrible flop—yet he routinely labeled writers, producers, actors and movie executives idiots. Labeling others is easy. Accomplishment, not so easy.

At one time or another, you, too, may be labeled as an idiot. Because I am a firm, consistent, cautionary and critical voice to entrepreneurs about surrendering to the tyranny of technology, to peer pressure about its use, to popular but not necessarily deserving of investment online media, and because I famously refuse to carry a cell-phone or personally use the internet, I know well that I am viewed and gossiped about as a dinosaurish idiot by many – despite a growing body of evidence that peoples' productivity is often severely impaired by their indiscriminate adoption of each and every new social media activity and gadget, and despite a growing "underground" of top CEO's and business leaders and authors opting out. What others think of me is really unimportant to me, to the point that my profound disinterest in their approval or disapproval makes them very unhappy. In an earlier chapter, I spoke of the success-store's non-negotiable price tags. It's my experience that one of these price tags is being willing to be thought of poorly, one way or another, by many.

As I mentioned in this book's introduction, the "Washed Up Has-Been" label was sewn on Joan Rivers after the loss of her talk show and the suicide of her husband, and it was sewn on by her own agent and manager, many 'supposed' friends, and the media. Joan defied the label with grit, hard work, a willingness to go through any door of opportunity she could find, humor, talent and self-confidence. She refused to let her actions be limited or dictated by the label others were so eager to attach to her.

In preparation for another book, I did considerable research on Debbi Fields, founder of Mrs. Fields Cookies. She and I also appeared as speakers on several events together. Debbie is arguably one of the best known, most widely recognized, and most phenomenally successful women entrepreneurs of our time. But in the beginning she was labeled as an "empty-headed housewife" by her husband's business acquaintants, bankers, family, "friends", vendors and suppliers.

Fran Tarkenton, who I've gotten to know thanks to a number of Guthy-Renker Corporation projects, was labeled "too small to play in the NFL." Today's quarterbacks are still scrambling to catch up to some of his records. Doug Flutie, a collegiate football superstar, was labeled "too small" to play pro ball by the NFL. One year he was THE most valuable player—with his multi-million dollar arm—in the expanding Canadian Football League.

It seems that the world is eager to attach labels; too old… too young… too small… too big… too slow… too dumb… too clumsy… too inexperienced… too this-or-that. You've just about got to keep one eye open while you sleep because somebody may be sneaking up to try and label you.

It is important to note that successful people tend to defy their labels past and present with their actions. Unsuccessful people accept and conform to their labels, by their actions.

Chapter 9 – Ben Glass

You Can Learn About Success From This Teenage Boy

It doesn't matter how old you are, you can find success at any age. Zac Sunderland, the teenager who sailed around the world by himself, is a prime example.

Here are five principles of success that you can take from his remarkable story:

Perseverance

From the very moment Zac decided he wanted to sail around the world, he faced waters seemingly too treacherous to brave. He needed money for his expedition, so he started his campaign. It was an obstacle to raise money, but he wouldn't take no for an answer.

He kept seeking out sponsors—months of sending out letters, meetings with business representatives, and just getting ordinary people to believe in him. It is not every day one hears about a teenager circumnavigating the globe. Most do not readily take that kind of endeavor seriously, but because of his persistence he was able to get the money he needed.

Hard Work

Zac learned to stick with it. When the rubber met the road, he worked his hardest. Even though sponsors provided a fair portion of the finances for his voyage, he got a job to help pay for the rest, including his boat. His boat, aptly named Intrepid, did not come ready to sail around the world. Zac and his dad sometimes worked 16-hour days to completely renovate it. They completely gutted it—rewiring electrical, reworking the plumbing, installing new navigation-, meteorological-, and communication equipment. Zac made sure the boat was perfect. The hull was repaired and painted and the mast was even replaced with the help of a borrowed crane. All of these repairs and boat preparations took place while Zac was still trying to attain sponsors and money for his trip.

Experience

Obviously, Zac is not a typical boy with a dream. He had prepared most of his life to engage in an adventure as big as circumnavigating the globe. Experience is needed to sail the high seas—and Zac had it. He grew up constantly surrounded by water and boating. The Sunderland family had faith in him, knowing that his prior sailing experience was more than sufficient to meet the challenges that would come along on his journey. Even Zac's first house was a boat, and his father had quite a bit of knowledge to offer, since he had spent a lifetime in the business. Because Zac's dad was constantly up, down, and all around the coast of California, Zac was able to learn valuable lessons that would prepare him for his journey ahead.

Quick Thinking

Being knowledgeable about sailing only goes so far, though. It takes a certain special something to be able to think quick on your feet about immediate, difficult decisions. This skill is something that Zac has seemed to master.

Once, while on his 'round-the-world voyage, Zac's radar didn't pick up an ocean liner. Before he knew it, his 36-foot boat was up against a giant ship. Thinking quickly, he diverted his course and avoided a collision that could have wrecked him and Intrepid.

There were numerous other occasions that parts and machinery on his boat went haywire, but Zac knew what to do. It is this attribute that has made Zac capable of withstanding the pressure and difficulties that come with success.

Self-Reliance

"When you're the only one in a situation, there's no one to help you; you have to be reliant on yourself." This is what Zac told Success Magazine in its November 2009 issue. He is not only experienced, tenacious, and smart, he is also confident—something absolutely necessary for true success. Even though he was running on little sleep, eating miniscule amounts of food, and captaining a ship single-handedly, the confidence and strength he had inside got him all the way around the world. We can all learn a lot about success from Zac.

This article first appeared in the August, 2010, edition of the BenGlassLaw newsletter.

Chapter 10 – Dan Kennedy

Why Even Smart, Talented, Skilled People Fail To Get What They Want From Their Lives

If a fire erupts in a crowded theater, most everybody will leap up and hurry from their seats in mad stampede toward exits. But how many people, on arrival, take notice of the location of exits and choose their seats to allow best access to them if needed?

When a need or desire occurs—a leaky roof worsening with each rain or a new car or home to buy—everybody digs into their finances to figure out how they might assemble the money or credit required for that purchase. How many people, do you suppose, have a complex portfolio of pre-determined goals, know the financial requirements of those goals, and benchmark and track their income, savings and wealth progress day by day or week by week, month by month, year by year?

Most business owners report to work at their place of business quite reliably. But how many arrive with a detailed agenda for the day, including key objectives, pre-set start and stop times for meetings, phone calls and tasks, and a sense of urgency about successfully completing that agenda? Most business owners also advertise, market and promote, but how many do so by a marketing plan and calendar devised for the entire year ahead?... employing systematic outreach for new customers, follow-up on unconverted leads or visitors who don't purchase, follow-up with customers?

(Since training, consulting and coaching on marketing strategies and systems has been my primary role for over 30 years, I can tell you with authority that the overwhelming majority of business owners as well as salespeople live and die by random acts of sales and marketing, have more holes in the bottom of their buckets than buckets, and can't diagram their step-by-step system for maximum monetization of every lead, every customer, every opportunity in their business if you offer them a million dollars for the drawing. They permit randomness in every nook and cranny, from the way their phones are answered to what happens after an appointment with no sale to—everything.)

Almost everybody exerts effort. And in that sense, almost everybody takes action. Yet, the population in general and every sub-population within it organizes itself into a pyramid, with—consistently—1% at its peak, another 4% near its top, 15% doing well, then a precipitous drop to a big hunk of about 50% that I call The Mediocre Majority, then 30% barely in the game at all. This tells us that **action or activity alone has little connection to success and failure.** There are many different kinds of action, activity and effort. For example, in the above paragraphs I wrote of 'organized effort.' Top professional athletes have carefully organized diet and exercise regimens connected to very specific objectives. Most regular guys show up at the gym and take whatever machine's available. Eat randomly, depending on what's in the 'frig, cooked and put on the dinner table in front of them, or where their buddies decide to go for lunch. Everybody has worked out and everybody has eaten, but in the pyramid of fitness, there are 1% in amazing condition, 4% in damned good condition, 15% within the range of good condition, then a precipitous drop. So it is with income, with sales or entrepreneurial or other for-profit personal performance, with companies, with wealth. With any kind of success you want to examine.

Activity asks only one question: *are you working?* Productivity asks many more complicated and, well, productive questions, in order to break the Work-Money Link. *Are you working in the environment most conducive to your success? On the right priorities? In ways that utilize your strengths? On your agenda—or others? With measurement and accountability?* And on and on and on. Woody Allen famously said that just showing up accounted for 33% of all success. But it's that other 66% that gets complicated. And **it is the willingness to manage self and business with a complicated structure and system for success that differentiates** the 1% from the 4%; combined, the 5% from the next 15%; and combined again, the 20% from the 80%.

THE ULTIMATE SUCCESS SECRET

One of the things to decide, going forward, is how demanding you are going to be of yourself as well as of everyone around you. I have written entire books about these two subjects, which I urge getting and reading: *No B.S. Time Management For Entrepreneurs* and *No B.S. Ruthless Management Of People And Profits*. These books are confrontational, and will challenge you.

After speaking for several hours at a seminar about the subjects of productivity, self-management, accomplishment and autonomy, a woman approached me, frowning. She said that, while she agreed with everything I said *in principle*, and certainly *wanted* the kind of autonomy and success and wealth I'd described, surely there had to be a way to have it all *without sacrificing* her spontaneity and being so regimented in managing herself and her affairs. She didn't like the rigidity of my approach. I told her that when I flew home that evening by private jet, I had a specific destination at which I intended to arrive safely, without incident, on time, and I hoped my pilots weren't committed to spontaneity. As a shareholder in a portfolio of companies, I chose none based on them having CEO's committed to spontaneity. I'm reasonably confident that Trump often feels like wearing khaki slacks, no socks, and a T-shirt, but he is never seen in public wearing anything but the specific business uniform he has found effective and made a trademark. He is not at all spontaneous about wardrobe, just throwing on whatever he's in the mood to wear. I made no less than a million dollars a year as a speaker for many years, performing a carefully scripted, tested, timed sales speech with such precision you could set your watch by the word. I did *not* go out there and spontaneously talk about whatever was on my mind any particular day. I make no less than a million dollars a year as a direct-response copywriter and as an influential writer with six newsletters, writing by pre-determined formulas and checklists and disciplines, *not* by spontaneously writing if, when inspired, on whatever topic captures my interest.

Sorry, kiddo, but everything in the success-store does have a price tag attached; written in ink; non-negotiable.

There are lots of ways to defend failure behavior. Spontaneity is one of many. Characterizing yourself as "an idea person" who just "isn't good at" organization, discipline and implementation is another. There are even personality assessment tests you can take that will validate such a precept, so you have independent verification of your deficiency. But try depositing *that* in the bank, or buying your dream home, or funding your retirement with it. You can't walk up to the cash register in the success-store with any of that as accepted currency.

Ultimately, there are only two choices to be made. To continue and endlessly, creatively defend failure behavior OR determine what success behavior is and re-train yourself to practice it—and even to like it.

I used to love everything about drinking and drinking to excess. I used to love a diet of Mexican food, pizza and pasta, bread, and my favorite breakfast food was doughnuts. I was guilty of swinging into Dunkin' Doughnuts to get two or three to eat in the car en-route to the airport, then having another with coffee at the airport. And I shared President Bush #1's attitude about broccoli. I have re-trained myself to eat a markedly different diet and to avoid alcohol altogether. As I was writing the revisions for this book, I found need to make it even more strict, and I can't honestly say I prefer my new diet versus the old one, nor that I love its rigid restrictions, but I recognize it is the non-negotiable price written in ink for not being fat and woefully unhealthy, for being fit enough to engage in a physically demanding sport as a professional, for managing diabetes without side effect laden drugs and injections—for success. I am 45 pounds lighter than at my worst weight, I've shed it, I've kept it off for years now, only by keeping it off everyday, every meal, every snack.

You can re-train yourself for any sufficiently motivational purpose. Whatever the source you wish to credit, humans have capacity for re-invention denied all other living creatures. But not if you cling to old defenses for existent, failure behavior. You can accomplish just about anything you might set out to do, but not without sacrifice of other things. Sorry, but everything in the success-store has a price tag attached; written in ink; non-negotiable. Every road to success has a toll booth and a non-negotiable toll.

Ultimately, forward progress is pretty darned simple. It is about getting productive and profitable things done, as quickly as can be (without sloppy haste that causes undue waste or dangerous recklessness), as consistently as can be. Speed matters. Constancy matters. DONE matters a lot. Until DOING becomes DONE, accomplishment is merely an intent and a hope; there is only activity.

If you watch most people, you will realize they are reacting, not proactively determining. They are going through every day like the little metal ball inside an old-fashioned pinball game machine, bouncing and spinning about as the different paddles flip up and hit them. At the end of each such day they are exhausted, and no wonder. At the end of each period of evaluation, month, year, they are disappointed. Random response to external stimuli rarely produces real accomplishment, and to whatever degree it does, it occurs with low efficiency. The flippers in the game can be anything from compulsively checking and indiscriminately responding to e-mails and texts to dealing with whatever customer appears rather than prospecting or marketing to bring best customers in by appointment. The list of every flipper that people let bounce them about would be as long as this book. It's up to you to identify all in your life and get control of them. That raises its own questions – notably will you? and then, when? There is only one correct answer to that second question, and it is the secret of this entire book.

Chapter 11 – Ben Glass

Time, There Never Seems To Be Enough Of It

Are you one of those people who constantly complains that you don't have enough time to get things done? Do you possibly blame the fact that you live in a major city or nearby for the time pressures that you have? Do you, in fact, surrender to other people's perceptions about the crush of time and figure that "this is the way it is supposed to be?" Here are the irrefutable facts about time:

- You have as much time as anyone else in the world; 24 hours a day, by last count

- How you spend your time is based entirely on the choices you make

- Your decision as to who and what you allow into your life determines whether you have "enough" time.

Ben's "Superman" Tips for Capturing More Time:

1. Keep a time log for five days. Record everything you do in 15- minute increments. Be honest. You will be surprised to see where your time actually goes.

2. Set aside 30 minutes (or wake up 30 minutes early one day) and write down your list of what you value most. I'll bet that "time with family vastly outranks both "surfing the internet" and "watching the latest/greatest TV show."

3. Looking at your time log, make a list of those things you actually spent time on that have absolutely no relationship to your top five. Ditch them or delegate them.

4. Ditch any device you have that gives people unfettered access to you. Yes, that's your Blackberry™ or other device that says to the world "interrupt me at any time—go ahead—I wasn't doing anything productive anyway!"

5. Don't be guilted into giving away your time to everyone who asks for it. YES, we all have causes that are on our top five "most important thing to do with our lives," but otherwise, learn to say NO to mindless and mind-numbing committee meetings run by and for people who get total enjoyment out of dragging you down into their "I have no time" mire.

This article first appeared in the August, 2008, edition of the BenGlassLaw newsletter.

Chapter 12 – Dan Kennedy

Take Action To Get Paid

One of the most interesting metaphysical authors, Stuart Wilde, says "When they show up, *bill 'em*." What does that mean? It actually refers as much to overriding attitude as to business policy.

One meaning is to <u>properly value your time</u>. If you do not place a high value on your time, I can promise you no one else will. Yet, the one thing we all have an equal amount of is time. Everybody starts out each day with 24 hours to invest as wisely as possible, for profit, for joy, for the benefit of others. The richest man in the world gets not a minute more to work with than does the poorest beggar on the street. But you can bet everything you've got that he thinks about that time differently, feels about that time differently, allocates that time differently, and has an entirely different intellectual, emotional, physical and actual experience with time than does the beggar. There's the rub; to get from poor to rich, you have to adopt the attitudes about time of the rich.

Another meaning, a bigger one, is to value yourself.

When I first started in the 'success education business', one of the few people in the country who was consistently effective at selling self-improvement audio programs direct, face to face, to executives and salespeople gave me what turned out to be very, very good advice—he said: "Don't waste your time trying to sell these materials to the people who need it most. They won't buy it. You should focus on selling to successful people who want to get even better." Over the years, I've demonstrated the validity of this to myself a number of different ways. And I've developed an explanation for it. There is what I now call "the self-esteem Catch-22 loop" at work here: in order for a person to invest directly in himself, which is what buying self-improvement materials is, he has to place value on himself, i.e. have high self-esteem, but if he has such high self-esteem, he is probably already doing well and does not have a critical need for this type of information; he will get marginal improvement out of it; but the person who needs it most does not place much value on himself, i.e. has relatively low self-esteem which prohibits him from buying, believing in or using self-improvement materials.

At a very practical level, I see this "value hang-up" surface all the time with entrepreneurs, authors, speakers, consultants, doctors dealing with fees and prices. I understand it. I still remember the first time I quoted a client $15,000,00 to develop a direct-mail campaign for him, held my breath, and instantly thought to myself *"Geez, Kennedy, a lot of people work all year to make that much money. What business do YOU have asking for that for a few days' work? Who do you think you are anyway?"* But here's the amazing thing:

the world largely accepts YOUR appraisal of your value, and just about everybody under-values and under-prices their contributions.

My good friend Rodney Tolleson was very active for a handful of years in the practice management business, providing doctors of chiropractic with a comprehensive collection of business-building services, training and counseling. I worked with him doing many of the seminars. We both discovered that these "professionals" were no different than anyone else; they had incredible mental and emotional blocks about charging what they and their service were worth. Although his company provided them with enormously helpful technical, management and marketing assistance and tools, the greatest income leaps were achieved by focusing on the doctors' beliefs about worth and value—"practice esteem" and "self esteem." There was more 'fee resistance' in the doctors' minds than in the public's. And all their actions relative to promoting the practice, stimulating referrals, setting, asking for and promptly collecting fees, insisting on compliance with recommendations were governed —hindered—by their surprisingly low self appraisals.

A 'No B.S. Marketing Letter" Subscriber & Insider's Circle™ Member Hits The Nail On The Head

I'm fortunate to have tens of thousands of Insider's Circle Members™ and Subscribers who are bright, curious, innovative, and contributive, so ours is more of a continuing dialogue than just my publishing a newsletter. One such Member is David Garfinkel, the President of a consulting firm named 'Let Your Clients Do Your Selling.' When I got into the final stages of this book, I invited my Members to submit their ideas about "the ultimate secret of success." David's suggestion was most interesting. And, while it does not name "the ultimate secret", it does hit the nail on the head about the chief obstacle to benefiting from that secret.

David said, "After all the smoke clears, it gets down to one thing—one limiting belief—one self-concept that, once revamped, will set you off on a permanent success trajectory, I think that's different for each of us, but it's usually a personal version of the feeling 'Yes, I really CAN succeed.'"

I agree. For more than 15 years, I have explained that we live inside two boxes:

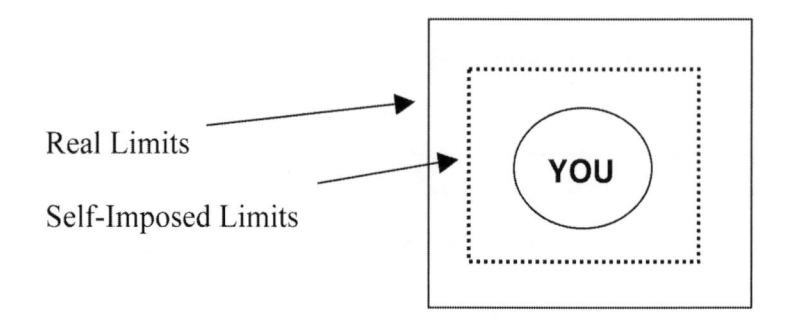

Real Limits

Self-Imposed Limits → YOU

The solid, outer boundary represents REAL LIMITS, and we all have some real limits. For a time, the oldest active player in the NFL was Vince Evans, a back-up quarterback for the Oakland Raiders – playing capably at age 39, the year I was when I wrote this book. More recently, Brett Favre came within a couple plays of putting the Minnesota Vikings in the Super Bowl as the oldest starting quarterback in the NFL. Still, I really CAN'T go try out and make the roster of an NFL team unless I buy one, like the Warren Beatty character in the movie Heaven Can Wait. Even if I diligently trained non-stop for the next 12 months, I still couldn't do it. I didn't play in high school or college (I didn't go to college), I'm not big on exercise, I have a bad back made worse by serious injuries while driving in harness races, a bad knee, horrible eyesight. There is a REAL limit making my playing quarterback in the NFL impractical.

As of now, you can't do business on Mars. That's a REAL limit. (Although there is an enterprising fellow who has sold thousands of deeds to imaginatively named lots of land on Mars at, as I recall, $1,000.00 each, by mail-order. Also outer-space related, the bombastic promoter Richard Branson has collected fee deposits from a lot of people for their flights on his to-be-built, who-knows-when rocket ships.)

There are REAL LIMITS on what you may want to do.

But way inside that solid line, real boundary, is the dotted line. The dotted line represents the **SELF-IMPOSED LIMITS**. This is a much smaller box we build around ourselves. It's made up of "IF", "CAN'T, "IMPOSSIBLE" inaccurately applied, of negatives in "The Big 4 Of Life": Self-Esteem, Self-Image, Self-Confidence and Self-Discipline. But David's suggestion adds a new wrinkle to all this; that there is ONE "dot" on this dotted line that is bolder, blacker, bigger and more significant than all the others... and that when you bust through it, the entire dotted line box disappears.

In monetary terms, that dotted line certainly controls how much value you place on yourself, your time, your know-how and your services, how much you dare demand, and how much you get. Anytime you push that box out, you automatically increase your income. Now I would suggest that the biggest leap can come from pushing against it at the point where it seems strongest.

"Abundance" Doesn't Care

Liberals constantly try to demonize exceptional ambition and achievement. This follows a liberal theme that the economy is and must be "win-lose" if one person gets "too rich" that must somehow force others to become poor or poorer. This kind of class divisiveness may be necessary politics for the liberals, but it is economic nonsense. And, unfortunately, this is one of the ways people build up guilt about striving for and achieving extraordinary successes.

Foster Hibbard often talked about two men going down to the ocean, one with a teaspoon, the other with a bucket, each taking away the amount of water he chooses to take away. The ocean, however, doesn't care. The ocean doesn't care if you come down there with a teaspoon, bucket or tanker truck. The ocean is a miraculously replenishing, unlimited resource. That represents ABUNDANCE. And Abundance doesn't care either. It matters not to Abundance whether you tap into it a little or a lot. Your "withdrawals" don't diminish anyone else's opportunities nor do they damage the total amount of available abundance. It is infinite. Infinite! And the only limits on "your share" are placed on you by you.

∼

WHAT YOU ARE
WILLING
TO ACCEPT
IS
WHAT YOU GET.

∼

Chapter 13 – Ben Glass

The Art Of Failure

A recent article in *Forbes* magazine reminded me of a saying that I am fond of. In the article, Anne Sweeney, co-chair, Disney Media Networks, is quoted as saying that when she saw a plaque that said *What would you attempt to do if you knew you could not fail?* it stopped her in her tracks and changed her life. She says the quote resonated with her and she wanted to apply the saying to her life. She called it "the best advice she ever got." Most importantly, she took action on her thoughts.

How many times have you NOT done something that you thought you might like to do because you were afraid of failing? Maybe you were afraid of what others might say or think about you. Often, we don't do things we would like to do just because we get "negative" feedback from those around us when we mention the idea.

When Sandi and I first started our adoption journey with Kevin, we often found ourselves frozen in fear. There were many fears: Travel to China; dealing with cleft lip and palate; we already had five children; we got negative feedback from some. We literally had taken a sheet of paper and drawn a line down the middle, with "reasons for" and "reasons against" listed when we sat down at our church one Sunday and our pastor gave a sermon entitled, "What would you do if you knew you could not fail?" The message of that sermon changed our lives forever. We sat there, quietly weeping, as the message of the sermon emboldened us and we decided to make a decision that was not based on the fear of failure!

I'd like to embolden you. What is failure itself but a perception of the outcome of an event? What person of "success" do you know who has not "failed" over and over again? Did I "fail" the marathon because 8,871 people finished in front of me? Did Bill Gates "fail" when he flunked out of Harvard? (This is not an excuse to not study, by the way.) The only true "failure" in life is not taking the God-given talents you were born with and using them or letting your mind talk you out of a venture or opportunity because you envisioned what might happen if all did not go perfectly.

This article first appeared in the November, 2008, edition of the BenGlassLaw newsletter.

Chapter 14 – Dan Kennedy

Take Action To Win Over Worry

I have had a great many misfortunes in my life—but only about half as many as I have painfully anticipated.

Worry can create physical illnesses, stress and fatigue. Worry robs you of your competence and confidence. Many people are literally immobilized by worry.

Yet, as destructive as we know worry to be, and as unnecessary as worrying often proves to be, most people still let worry into their lives virtually every day. Ironically, we give our worries power by thinking about them. The more you worry about something, the more power worry itself gains over you. Even small worries can amass enormous power if you let them. Dr. Edward Kramer observed: **"A penny held to the eye blocks the sun."**

So, how do you eliminate worry from your life?

I'm not sure you can eliminate it. Worry is often the starting point of constructive, creative thought. But you can reduce its time consumption and influence in your life.

You can temporarily do it with chemicals. Booze. Prescription, over-the-counter or street drugs. Personally, I used the drink-to-coma method myself, for several years. The problem with that is, when you return to the real world, the things you were worrying about are there waiting for you, and you're further handicapped in dealing with them by the hangovers and other physical debilitation. This kind of escape yields no real benefit and has its own added costs. I can't speak to the drug thing, as I've never tried any street drugs and very rarely even swallow a Tylenol. But I can talk about alcohol from experience, and I'll only, briefly say this: if you find yourself knocking back a few every day, everything you tell yourself about not having a problem is crap. You've got a problem. NOT a solution; a problem. If you protect it and continue with it, it will eventually destroy your business or career, an important relationship, your health or land you in jail. If you cannot quickly kick this habit alone, get help.

THE only real antidote for worry is action.

Decision is the empowering opposite of worry. When you take action to solve a problem, you take power away from the problem, and you gain power. For every source of worry and anxiety, there is usually a list of a number of potentially helpful actions. If you'll get involved in making that list and acting on all the items on the list, worry will be eliminated; it cannot co-exist with such constructive action.

I recently read an article about a CEO of a huge company, on the brink of financial ruin, presented with the fact that they had only enough cash to operate the business for another three days. "What then," he asked, "are we going to spend it on?" He was instantly moving on to actions, not worry.

If you find yourself too frequently immobilized by worry, I have a book to recommend: W. Clement Stone's *The Success System That Never Fails*. Pay particular attention to his discussion of the sudden termination of his right to represent a particular company; the end of a business he had struggled mightily to build; an eminent and apparently unmanageable threat to everything he had and everything he had worked for; and how he reacted to it.

But—what about the problem you cannot take any action to resolve? First of all, there's rarely any situation that defies all action. But, for the sake of conversation, let's assume that you are up against something so tough that, at least at the moment, there is absolutely nothing you can do, no action you can take. If that is the case, then the only thing you can do is set that problem aside entirely and take action on some other matter or project that you can do something about.

The ONLY antidote for worry is action.

What about worrying about what others think? A great deal of unhappiness comes from people pursuing and achieving others' goals instead of their own. When I was a kid, one of our neighbors, Ralph F., created a great deal of unhappiness for himself, his wife and his five sons by obsessing over his sons' disinterest in taking over the family business. I wonder how many kids buckle under to such pressure and achieve the goals their parents' set for them—and wind up wishing they hadn't. Working to achieve others' goals set for you, to meet others' expectations, to satisfy others' definitions, that is what you do when you worry about what others think.

My friend, the late Herb True, had moved from the academic world to a very successful career in professional speaking, and could have continued to enjoy a growing, exceptional income, create and market cassette albums, author bestselling books and accumulate wealth. He chose not to. Herb chose to cut his business back to taking just a few speaking engagements a year so he could return to teaching at Notre Dame. When he did so, I know that many of his peers and friends thought he'd lost his marbles. Or gotten too old to compete. Or had the business pass him buy. None of those things were true. But regardless of what anybody else or everybody else thought, Herb chose to pursue his goals. The result was one of the most contented but invigorated, happy and fulfilled individuals I know or have ever observed.

Oh, and you'd probably be surprised (disappointed?) if you knew how little others think about you. Most people have their hands full dealing with their own lives. They ponder yours a lot less than you probably assume. But regardless of how little or great the world's interest is in how you choose to live your life, "sooner or later you stand in your own space." The cure for worry over others' opinions is taking action that satisfies you and, as a result, increases your sense of control, feeling of power, self-confidence and self-esteem. Others can never gift you with self-esteem or peace of mind. These are products of your own actions.

Chapter 15 – Ben Glass

Mom And Dad, Don't Let Your Kids See You Whine

Recently, Fairfax County Public Schools have been contemplating having the high school kids start later. Kelsey, my junior at Robinson, gets on the bus at 6:35 in the morning. A recent article in the local newspaper quoted some parents who were supportive of the change and said things like. "Johnny doesn't want to get out of bed that early" or "When I get up with Johnny that early, *I can't find anything else to do after he leaves for the bus because no one else is up.*"

As you might guess, I thought that this was ridiculous. (So did Kelsey and a bunch of her friends, all of whom are involved in after-school activities and lead busy, productive lives.)

Here's the letter I wrote to the editor: Editor: The amount of whining by parents complaining about the "early start" that many students have to their school day was shocking. Since when is it a bad thing that a 13-year old goes to bed "on her own volition" when she is tired? One mother complained that while she got up "early" with her children and tried to get started on some household business she "couldn't because no one else was available so early in the morning." It's incredible that she could not think of one thing to do at that hour that did not involve other people.

Two quick thoughts: 1) I'll bet that if we followed these children (and often, their parents) around for just five days, and documented what they are doing with their lives every fifteen minutes, we would find a lot of wasted time. Text messaging with friends, updating your Facebook "profile" and watching reruns of American Idol do not a productive society make. 2) I would also bet that if instead of school these children (and again, their parents) were getting up to head to a job which required that they do moderately complex reading, writing and arithmetic and that the show up on time every day in return for a pay scale of $100 an hour, that they would figure out a way to do it, especially if they only got paid if they showed up on time and did productive work.

Children who see their parents whine about an "early start" in a public newspaper will be some of the same children who are taking mommy and daddy with them along to job interviews later. This is not the kind of self-discipline that America was built on.

This article first appeared in the February, 2009, edition of the BenGlassLaw newsletter.

Chapter 16 – Dan Kennedy

Take Action When Your 'Inner Voice' Speaks

About 50 years ago or so, an expectant mother took a $500.00 risk and placed a little ad in "*Seventeen Magazine*" for a new purse monogrammed with the customer's initials. She believed in her idea and acted on it, even though $500.00 was a great deal of money for her at the time, even though she had no market research to support it, even though she had no business experience. Her little ad produced $32,000.00 in orders. The Lillian Vernon Company matured to selling more than 150-million dollars of merchandise every year, ultimately sold for a queenly price.

In a speech to the New York Venture group on May 17, 1990, Lillian Vernon said, "I make quick decisions. I take chances, relying on what I consider 'my golden gut.'".

She went on to say: "Growing from a million dollar to a multi-million dollar company involved areas such as finance, list management, computers and large-scale production realms beyond my expertise. I tried to cover my shortcomings by surrounding myself with experienced veterans of large corporate cultures, usually from outside the direct marketing industry. There were so few direct marketers in the early 1970's that I filled my ranks with managers from different walks of life who generally were very savvy to the ways of big business—and most of them almost killed us. I don't want to generalize but some of the corporate executives I hired just couldn't make a decision. They took analysis to the point of paralysis. Every consideration had to first be studied by a committee. In my business, sending a good idea to a committee is like sending Rip Van Winkle to a slumber party. I hate more than anything to wake up and find that one of my competitors is already doing something I was planning on." For many years, Lillian Vernon continued picking winning products for her catalogs, often trusting her 'golden gut' and making fast decisions. Other great mail-order catalog merchants including my friend Joe Sugarman, J. Peterman—made famous in the Seinfeld TV shows as Elaine's boss, and featured in my book, *No B.S. Marketing to the Affluent*, and Roger Horchow have these two things in common: the "knack" for spotting a promotable product and the trust in their own intuition and instincts to act. Without the second thing, the first wouldn't be of much value.

Confident decisiveness is one of the most prized qualities in the business world. All great leaders exhibit it. People naturally respond to such a person. It is easy for the decisive individual to inspire trust and cooperation. Where does this kind of confident decisiveness come from? Call it what you will: intuition, the golden gut, the inner voice, insight – most exceptionally successful people admit to listening to a secret, inner advisor.

A Few Thoughts About "Insight"*

"The mind can only proceed so far upon what it knows, and can prove. There comes a point where the mind takes a leap—call it intuition or what you will—and comes out on a higher plane of knowledge." – Albert Einstein

My friend and speaking colleague Lee Milteer wrote an outstanding book, Success Is An Inside Job, and I thought excerpts from its chapter on *"Intuition: Your Secret Talent"* would be appropriate here:

"It is interesting that in our western culture we seem to comprehend almost all of our experiences through the logical, linear, analytical thinking process. We use words to communicate this kind of thinking. Because words are our way of understanding our world, we've almost forgotten we have an intuitive, creative part of ourselves. We're not trained to say I FEEL but rather I THINK. If we deny and cut off our intuition, then we get trapped by concepts learned through our programmed minds. Yesterday's learned beliefs (alone) cannot solve today's challenges or enable us to capitalize on tomorrow's opportunities.

Today more and more successful people—executives, artists, entrepreneurs—are realizing that making decisions is not an exclusive function of the analytical left side of the brain. You must now use the intuitive and creative right side of your brain as well. You must have an integration of analytical and intuitive thinking. This is commonly referred to as *'whole brain thinking.'* Dr. Jonas Salk said, 'A new way of thinking is now needed to deal with our present reality. Our subjective responses (intuitive) are more sensitive and more rapid than our objective responses (reasoned). This is the nature of the way the mind works. We first sense, then we reason why.'

I suggest that you have some fun in your life and start testing your intuitive abilities. When the phone rings, ask yourself who it is before you answer—see how many times you're right. When waiting for an elevator, guess which one will come first. There are dozens of small games you can play with yourself to strengthen your abilities. Your 'intuitive muscle' gets stronger as you use it. Then, when you need your intuition, you will feel more confident in using it.

In his book *'The Intuitive Edge'*, Philip Goldberg noted '... astonishing speed with which the truly intuitive mind can bring together bits of information only remotely related in time and meaning to form the sudden hunch or whispered feeling that we call intuition.' Conrad Hilton, who was well known for using his intuition in his hotel business, wrote 'I know when I have a problem and have done all I can to figure it out, I keep listening in a sort of inside silence till something clicks and I feel a right answer.'"

Here are some of Lee's Action tips for Encouraging your intuition:

- Listen to your body; that's why we call intuition a 'gut' feeling. The solar plexus is a large network of nerves located behind the stomach and is said to be the seat of emotion. You can have an accurate, gut-level reaction to many situations.

- Allow yourself to re-define the problem frequently; writing out the problem gives you the opportunity to see the problem from a different perspective.

- Allow yourself to play. You don't have to be sitting in your office to come up with creative and intuitive solutions. Take a walk, feed the birds, play hooky for an hour and then come back to work on the problem.

- Take action on your insights. Start investigating with the approach of "will this hunch logically work?"

Two of the self-help pioneers that I've long been a serious student of, Napoleon Hill and Dr. Edward Kramer, both promote reliance on insight and intuition. I don't often talk about it, but I often act on little "flashes" that come to me seemingly out of the blue. I'll give you an example:

Some years back, at a seminar about direct marketing where I was a featured speaker, one of the attendees was a long-time subscriber and 'student' of mine, a chiropractor in private practice, and the owner of a practice management company consulting with other doctors. During the two days, I heard him talk about his goals for expanding his second business. On the flight home, a "flash" came—I'll bet he would buy my SuccessTrak business, centered around my 'Practice-Building Secrets Newsletter' for chiropractors. Prior to that "flash" I had not been thinking about selling that business, although I was gradually recognizing that it was no longer a good fit with my other interests and activities, was being neglected, and was losing value. As I thought about this "flash", I developed the argument in my mind for the synergy between this doctor's management business and goals and why my business would be worth more to him than to me. Most importantly – let me say it again: *most importantly,* immediately on my arrival at home, I generated a letter to him suggesting the deal. It was consummated to my satisfaction in a matter of weeks.

For me, this is not at all unusual. These "flashes" frequently occur, I frequently act on them quickly, and I frequently benefit as a result. Consequently, I'm a believer in the role of "intuition" in otherwise hard-nosed, tough-minded, pragmatic business environments. And I find information on the subject, such as that Lee has assembled in her book, of great value.

(You can find information about Lee's books at leemilteer.com)

How To Use The Miraculous "Dominant Thought Principle" To Energize Your Inner Advisor

I will try to tell this true-life story as briefly as possible: in my hometown of Akron, Ohio, a prominent judge, respected citizen, family man, wound up on the front page of *The Akron Beacon Journal* and in prison, as a child molester. This was more than 30 years ago; we were still shocked by such things. He was asked how a man like him could wind up in such a horrible situation. He described a "process"— he said, "One day, years ago, I was out watering my lawn, a little girl in a sundress went by and for a fleeting millisecond I thought about what it would be like with her—then, of course, I pushed it from my mind. But a year or so later, at a mall, another little girl, and I held the thought for maybe a minute." He went on to mention another incident, a few minutes of thought. Another incident, 15 or 20 minutes of thought. "Then one day," he said, "I woke up and found it was all I was thinking about. For days, it dominated my thoughts. Then I did it."

This is a NEGATIVE example of the amazing power of Dominant Thought.

After 20 years of intense research into what made super successful people tick, Napoleon Hill wrote: "Our brains become magnetized with the dominating thoughts which we hold in our minds, and by means which no man is familiar, these magnets attract to us the forces, the people, the circumstances of life which harmonize with the nature of our dominating thoughts."

I know this to be true, personally, in its positive and its negative application.

When you come to grips with this Dominant Thought Principle, you have the "supercharger device" for dramatically accelerating the achievement of any objective; instead of taking weeks, months or years to move from first, fleeting thought to dominant thought, deliberately utilize dominant thought—because the lapse of time between dominant thought, action and achievement is minimal. All the time is taken up in getting to dominant thought. Very little time is required to get from dominant thought to reality.

Beyond this, dominant thoughts energize your Inner Advisor. Your dominant thoughts are your Inner Advisor's directives. Your dominant thoughts tell your Inner Advisor what to work on. Your Inner Advisor then jumps into action; mobilizes all the vast resources of your subconscious mind, your memory, your experience, your connection to universal intelligence. Then your Inner Advisor tells you precisely what to do, who to call, where to go and when to act, to get from dominant thought to reality as rapidly as possible. When you energize your Inner Advisor with deliberate dominant thought, you can trust and confidently, decisively act on the Advisor's recommendations.

Chapter 17 – Ben Glass

Change Can Happen, But It's Up To You To Take The Steps

Many people only dream of an exciting life and never really experience it. They sit in their offices or on their couches at home and think about far off places they'd like to go—but never do. Warren Macdonald has never been one of those people. He is always looking for adventure, finding beautiful things in the places he visits. One day in 1997, a kind of freedom he once had was ripped away.

After being trapped under a one-ton boulder for two days, Macdonald's life of adventure had seemingly come to an abrupt halt. He lost both of his legs from the knees up.

In the face of adversity, many people crack. Under pressure, they give up. But what most individuals would have considered being the end of their prior freedom, Macdonald only saw as another obstacle to overcome. He had the drive in him to carry on—and it carried him right on to being the first double amputee to climb to Africa's tallest peak, Mount Kilimanjaro. Macdonald has learned to face change and accept it even in the hardest of circumstances.

He shares this kind of thinking with others and has helped thousands of people bring change to their own lives. He wrote a short article entitled, *It's Your Move*, which includes his "five steps you can take to change your world today." These five steps are simple, easy, and yet so effective. Here is a brief summary of his steps:

Step One: Get rid of your TV.

Step Two: Get in shape.

Step Three: Eat organic, local food.

Step Four: Harness the power of your spending.

Step Five: Get to know your neighbors.

Macdonald is all for finding what is most important in life and striving to reach that. He notes that change is difficult for most and that it takes time, but what he has shown in his life is that obstacles and adversity are not an excuse to living a boring life. He has shown that it is the simple things that make a life worth living—a life that changes the world.

This article first appeared in the October, 2010, edition of the BenGlassLaw newsletter.

Chapter 18 – Dan Kennedy

Take Action To Profit From The Power Of Positive Association

Advertising agency empire-builder David Ogilvy established a tradition of welcoming new executives with a gift of five wooden dolls, each smaller than the other, one inside the other. When the recipient finally gets to the fifth little doll, the smallest doll, and opens it, he finds this message:

> *if each of us hires people who are smaller than we are, we shall become a company of dwarfs, but if each of us hires people who are bigger than we are, we shall become a company of giants.*

You can certainly take this beyond hiring. If you surround yourself and spend time with people who are 'smaller' than you are, you will stay as you are.

Take action to involve smart people in your projects. I am constantly impressed with how my clients, Greg Renker and Bill Guthy of the Guthy-Renker Corporation pull together project teams, invite outside experts and consultants to their company meetings, collect qualified opinions and data, and patiently explore differing viewpoints. They constantly apply Napoleon Hill's "mastermind principle." If you aren't familiar,

THE ULTIMATE SUCCESS SECRET

Guthy-Renker is the most successful producer of TV infomercials, and has used that media and just about every other media to build giant brands and businesses, including Proactiv® acne treatments, which began with a show featuring actress Judith Light, and as I'm writing this revised edition, many years later, has Justin Bieber, Katy Perry and Jennifer-Love Hewitt featured in the advertising. I've worked as a consultant and writer for Guthy-Renker off and on for more than 20 years, and have often been part of a specific project team, as well as a "mastermind participant" engaged in evaluating new product possibilities, devising advertising strategies and themes, and more. They view me as a smart fellow, and I appreciate the 20 year long compliment.

What's significant about this is that these men, who have built a billion dollar a year enterprise from scratch, have never reached that dangerous pinnacle of arrogance and isolation: thinking they are smarter than everybody else. Making a billion dollars a year *can* do that to you. But it hasn't done it to them. People of far lesser achievement do fall victim to this syndrome, and often discover that the slide down the back-side of the mountain happens a lot faster than did the climb up.

Take A Millionaire To Lunch

There are smart people readily accessible everywhere. You might seek out and tap retired and highly experienced executives or entrepreneurs in your field to assist and advise you. You might find successful people in your field, in other geographic areas, happy to share their experiences for the price of a lunch or dinner. My speaking colleague Jim Rohn urges people: "Take a millionaire to lunch." Jim says to buy him a big juicy steak, fine wine, then dessert and keep asking him questions, and keep listening carefully. And he observes that most people are too short-sighted to ever take this advice; hey, the guy's a millionaire?—let him buy his own steak. I'd add that most people take people to lunch who know less than they do, have less successful experience than they do, like a tennis player preferring the company of inferior players. You might find smart, helpful people through professional associations or at seminars and conferences. You might need to hire smart people to advise you or provide very specialized services for your business. Only one thing is certain; you won't find smart people if you do not take action to find them.

Most highly successful entrepreneurs are, these days, involved in several different formally organized mastermind groups, coaching programs and networking organizations, and it's likely that the person who put this book in your hands offers one or more such opportunities. There are also local 'Dan Kennedy Study Groups' and Chapters meeting in many cities nationwide, accessible via DanKennedy.com, with free guest passes usually available on request. Also, nearly every successful entrepreneur has at least a few key advisors he cheerfully pays to be part of his private brain trust. Even today's pro golfer, who appears to be playing a solo game, is actually very reliant on expert caddie, swing coach, sports psychologist and, off the course, financial adviser, attorney, licensing and brand management team, and publicist.

There are many good purposes served by such exposure and sharing of ideas and experiences among peers as well as the investing in solid, expert advice—not the least of which is avoiding unnecessary, costly mistakes.

At the American Booksellers Association, I ran into a young couple who had authored and published an excellent, unusual travel book. I had met them about 7 months earlier at a conference for self-publishers where I spoke. At that conference, they had asked me a few questions, but been resistant to advice they didn't like, clearly eager for someone to validate their own opinions, and even more clearly unwilling to pay for expert assistance. At this industry conference, they told me of having just appeared on a major national, network daytime talk show. But their book wasn't in stores and they never got their own 800# given out on the show, were not prepared to negotiate that with the show's producers, and were not prepared to hold their own as one of several guests on a panel—another of the guests monopolized the entire show. I certainly could have made sure they got their 800# shown and given out on the show, the calls handled, probably sold 5,000 or more books immediately by phone and collected three times that many inquiries, coached them in asserting themselves on the show, and otherwise helped them capitalize on this very difficult to get exposure. And I'm not the only one; there are any number of people very well qualified as advisors in such a situation. But they squandered a once-in-a-lifetime opportunity by being stubborn and by being cheap.

Every business, every occupation and every field has grown far too complex for one person to go it alone and capably handle every aspect of the activity. Insisting on doing EVERYthing yourself is very false economy.

In his first book, Lee Iacocca wrote about his "team of horses"—the mastermind group that turned Chrysler into a winner. In many instances, the existence and importance of a mastermind group within a business or organization goes unnoticed by most of the outside world. But behind most successes, there is between a 2-person and a 20-person mastermind alliance hard at work.

Now, here's a tricky part: you cannot listen only to advice you like and only to opinions that validate your own. Well, you can, but you'll almost certainly fail in most of your endeavors. Sometimes the most valuable person is the one with the courage to confront you and tell you "the Emperor has no clothes."

On the other hand, you need to take great care in choosing those people you test ideas on and solicit opinions from. At my seminars, I all too often hear from the person who had a "great idea", bounced it off a few friends, got talked out of it, only to subsequently see someone else come up with the same idea and go on to amass a fortune. It's a frequently told tale. In describing the proper makeup of a 'mastermind group'—the short list of those people you choose to routinely serve as your sounding boards—Dr. Napoleon Hill wrote: "We share nothing we plan to achieve with anyone except those who believe in us and who are in complete sympathy with our plans." This does not mean "yessers". No, we need good criticism. We need someone to point out the flaws and hazards we may overlook in our enthusiasm. But these people have to be truly eager for our success, confident of our abilities, progressive, innovative and optimistic in general, and possessing of successful, relevant experience and knowledge.

Walt Disney was more brutal and brief in his comments about others' opinions. He would typically ask ten people for their opinions and when all ten disliked one of his ideas he would rate that one as most worthy of investment. The great actor Peter Ustinov said, "If the world should blow itself up tomorrow, the last audible voice would be that of an expert saying: it can't be done."

Beware the expert who can only tell you what you canNOT do (or canNOT do without the expert). Look, instead, for the knowledgeable person who may point out flaws and question premises but can and will also suggest possibilities and improvements and, in general, is eager to figure out how you CAN accomplish your stated objectives.

Such people have to be "big" enough not to be jealous or envious of your success and accomplishments. They have to be smart enough to know what they do not know, and secure enough to admit it—a person with equally strong opinions about everything cannot be trusted. They must not fear the truth or shun reality, but they must be, overall, optimistic and positive-minded by nature. To paraphrase the title of Peter McWilliams' book, you cannot afford the luxury of a truly negative individual as a close advisor. And your collection of advisors should include people from 'inside' your particular field and from other, diverse fields.

Finally, in soliciting and considering opinions, there is a time to say "enough has to be enough" and then take action. I have often taken pains to correct peoples' picture of the entrepreneur as a wild-eyed risk-TAKER, defining the entrepreneur, instead, as someone who MANAGES risk. Obviously, the more information and worthwhile opinion you can assemble and consider before making an important decision, the better—however this balances out against a value-of-passing-time issue…the assembly and evaluation of information can become a never-ending pursuit in and of itself, with always one more person yet to be heard from, one more source yet to consult, one more piece of data to be obtained. If you're constantly seduced by the next piece of information to be uncovered, paralysis of analysis takes over.

The 3-Legged Stool Of Successful Achievement

Picture in your mind a 3-Legged Stool. If any one leg is missing, you can't sit on it; you topple over. One leg is no more important than the other. All three legs share exactly equal importance. Two without three is no better than one without two or even none. All three are vitally necessary. Their importance is evenly, perfectly balanced.

So, one of these legs is: INFORMATION. Another: ADVICE AND ASSOCIATION. The third is; DECISION AND ACTION.

Watch the pro football coach on the sidelines, the next time a game is on television. He has less than a minute between plays, to direct his offense. He has INFORMATION: in his hands, usually on pages attached to a clipboard, is a "game plan", including a collection of planned plays, all built on prior, careful analysis of information collected about the opposing team's strengths, weaknesses and behavior, as well as his own players' abilities, strengths and weaknesses. He has ADVICE AND ASSOCIATION: during the week before the game, most coaches confer with all their assistant coaches and players, and often by phone with a few trusted, little-mentioned advisors, like other coaches, retired coaches. During the game, he is getting input from assistant coaches in the 'skybox' above the field and from other assistants on the sidelines with him. He is getting instant feedback from the players—here's what happened… here's what I noticed on the last play. But then he still has less than a minute to arrive at DECISION. And, it doesn't matter whether it is what might be judged as a minimally important situation; the first play of the game; or a life-or-death situation, 4th and 4, two minutes left, down by a touchdown, he still has less than a minute. How would you do under similar pressure?

Of these three legs, ADVICE AND ASSOCIATION is the one you can and need to set up in advance, cultivate over time, and use on a daily basis. You'll do yourself a great favor by organizing your own network, your own "brain trust" or people whose judgment and support you can depend on. You'll do yourself another favor by joining formal mastermind groups and coaching programs run by reputable experts.

It's important to add that successful people are always… *actively*… on the look-out for valuable, authentic sources of information, advisors, individuals with useful experience to share, providers of new opportunities and services and allies who can somehow help them better reach their goals.

This trait exhibits itself in many actions, small and large. Such people do not merely order the occasional book from Amazon called to their attention by somebody else; they frequently visit a large bookstore and wander and browse, to find what they don't know exists, that might benefit them. They occasionally haunt used bookstores for the same purpose. When they attend conferences, they do not skirt the exhibit hall;

they diligently search it… they do not hang out only with friends; they actively engage new people… they do not skip sessions… and they routinely invest in offered resources they discover by being there. It is self-serving to point that last thing out, but I've been at this for 35 years, I'll wager the biggest steak in Texas that I intimately know a lot more made-from-scratch millionaire, multi-millionaire and even billionaire entrepreneurs than you do, and I can assure you: they are nearly compulsive buyers of success information.

They also go to pains and spare no expense in getting to THE source and securing one-to-one advice and coaching relevant to their objectives. I routinely have very smart and accomplished people flying to meet with me at one of my homes—I never travel to someone's place of business to consult—and, as of this writing, they pay the princely sum of $18,800.00 to sit with me from 9:00 AM to 4:00 PM and pick my brain. And I suspect I could charge more, but I'm not a greedy man. Many do this a couple times every year, year after year. Have I hypnotized or mesmerized them? Not at all. I am not the only beneficiary of their unending, active search for new, for better; their unending, active re-assessment of their own ideas, beliefs and modus operandi. It is their success behavior.

Chapter 19 – Ben Glass

Kindness Is Contagious

There are many reasons to be kind to others and a recent study gives you yet another one. According to a study by Nicholas Christakis, a physician and sociologist at Harvard University, and James Fowler, a social scientist at the University of California, San Diego, when people benefit from kindness, they "pay it forward." A movie came out years ago about this very concept.

The movie, *Pay It Forward,* followed a seventh grader who was prompted by his teacher to do something to make the world better. The boy created a plan to do three important favors for people who needed them. Instead of letting these individuals pay him back, he requested that they "pay it forward," by doing three favors for other people, and having them do the same.

While this may have only been a Hollywood movie, the recent study has found there to be merit in the movie's message. During the study, participants were asked to play a "public goods" game in which they gave money to others. What was interesting and encouraging about the findings is that the act of kindness or generosity that occurred in the first round tripled over the course of the experiment.

It's important to mention that the participants in the study didn't know each other before the game and they never played it more than once with the same person. The researchers of this study believe that "cooperative behavior cascades in human social networks," which basically means that kindness is contagious. Find some ways to help others this week. It doesn't have to be financial help; it can be a kind word or selfless action. You can read more about this study in the March 2010 online edition of Proceedings of the National Academy of Sciences.

This article first appeared in the June, 2010, edition of the BenGlassLaw newsletter.

Chapter 20 – Dan Kennedy

Take Action To (At Least) Double Your Paycheck

What you are about to read, I wrote for the very first edition of this book, in 2005. I have left it unchanged. It is even truer, more relevant, and more urgently in need of broad understanding today than then.

Here is the truth no politician, few economists, few teachers want to tell people, and that few people want to hear: certain jobs are only worth a certain, maximum number of dollars per hour, whether you've been there doing it for one year, ten years, or thirty years. Longevity does not necessarily merit more money because the individual's length of time on the job does not necessarily increase the real value of getting that job done. (Financial problems of big bureaucracies like the U.S. Postal system, the airline industry, the auto industry... our inability to compete in world markets... quality problems in our educational system... have a lot to do with the pressure on employers to pay more to people purely based on length of time on a job. Demagogue union leaders and politicians perpetuating this 100% false economy for their own gains have done irreparable harm to this country. Academics who wish to ignore how the economy really works and MUST really work have aided and abetted the fraud committed on the American public; on workers; on students being prepared for careers. The reason France has suffered with a 20% unemployment rate—yikes!—for over a decade is this foolish notion that jobs increase in value.)

As our economy is forced to acknowledge this uncomfortable reality in the years to come, there will be a great many bitter casualties.

However, hidden inside this uncomfortable truth, is the secret to increasing your income literally at will.

In his book, Earl Nightingale's *Greatest Discoveries,* Earl noted that "every field of human endeavor has its stars; all the rest in these fields are in a descending order of what we might call 'the **service-reward continuum**.'" He went on to point out that the reason some people earn more money than others is that they have made themselves more valuable. He observed that, for the most part, the size of a person's paycheck is determined by this question—*how difficult is he or she to replace?*

As I was writing this, I was listening to a roundtable debate on a Sunday morning news program about employment and productivity and security in America, and a young employee had this question for management and for unions—"How will you help me avoid losing my job in the future?" Well, you see, that's the wrong question. The unions try hard to protect their turf by answering it, and, as a result, they tell a big lie.

Management tries hard to answer it and, as a result, they lie. Government even sticks its nose in and tries to answer it and lies. The only real truthful response is to refuse to answer it at all. What this young man needs to do is go find a full-length mirror, sit down in a chair facing it, stare deeply into his own eyes, and ask himself: "What am I going to do to avoid losing my job in the future?" The key words are *"what am I going to do?"*—that is <u>the</u> question.

And here are the extension questions:

1. What am I going to do to increase my value in the marketplace?

2. What am I going to do to demonstrably increase my value to my current employer? (or clients, customers, patients.)

3. What am I going to do to increase my value to prospective future employers?

4. What am I going to do to make myself so valuable that I'm the least likely to be cut, the last to be cut?

Unfortunately, the most common responses are: "I don't have time"… "I can't afford to"… "my employer should"… "the government should"… Take evening classes and spend my own money? Hey, I already work hard all day. When I come home, I'm tired. And I can't afford to take classes. Besides, if these classes are going to give me skills I'll use on the job, my darned employer oughta pay for them. And I ought to get to take the classes during regular work hours. If I have to go to classes on my time, I should get time-and-a-half. Eric Hoffer wrote, "There are many who find a good alibi far more attractive than achievement."

I have sometimes been introduced, as a speaker, as The Professor Of Harsh Reality. Well, here is the harsh reality every adult should come to grips with as quickly as possible, every young person should be taught: one year, three years, and five years from now, the particular job (task) you do will not have appreciably increased in value. YOU will either have stayed the same in value or increased in value through your own initiative; that's the only way. If you have not increased in value and your job has not inherently increased in value, at some point, your employer can't or clientele won't pay more—regardless of inflation. It is at that point that your economic status shifts into reverse. Your income stagnates or declines. The gradual decline in your buying power as a consumer will prevent you from saving, investing and creating financial security or erode what you have already accumulated. And your vulnerability to lay-off, termination or replacement increases.

This is true of the self-employed, the business owner as well. If you are not increasing your value to your customers, if you are not making yourself indispensable to them all over again, every day, then you are declining in value to them. You are either increasing in value or declining in value.

How many people do you thing have this "add value" idea straight in their minds? Well, look around. One out of every ten adult Americans is on food stamps. 95% of the people reaching retirement age lack the financial resources to take care of their basic needs without all sorts of direct and disguised welfare. In most big companies, there are masses of people doing the very same jobs, the very same way year after year, even decade after decade, shocked when cheaper foreign labor or automation or some other 'replacement' boots them out on the street. Small business owners suddenly find themselves vulnerable when a major, mass retailer or chain or aggressive new competitor comes to town. How can these terrible things happen to "good people" in America?

Every one of these people has one very distinctive thing in common; from one year to the next, they have not taken any initiative, not done anything, not invested any money or time in increasing their own personal value. YOU need to look very closely at all these folks and avoid following their example at any and all cost. And if you really would like to double your paycheck, simply take action to triple your value; one of three things will absolutely, certainly happen: 1) your present employer will respond with raises, bonuses and advancement; 2) a new employer will find and grab you; or 3) you'll discover some entrepreneurial opportunity and move on to writing your own paycheck. And if you already own a business and would like to double your paycheck, simply take action to triple your value to your customers. Your compensation will always catch up to your value.

Chapter 21 – Ben Glass

Sowing Seeds Of Success

Many people believe that moving up the social ladder and changing their stars is impossible. They live mediocre lives, believing that a better life is unattainable. They go through life never improving their circumstances and simply living and struggling day to day.

For Dr. Alfredo Quiñones-Hinojosa, that was not acceptable. He saw that change, even though hard to come by, was possible to obtain. He knew that it was not impossible to go from being an immigrant farm worker to a renowned brain surgeon. Not only that, but he also saw that improvement does not come by waiting around for luck to strike, but by hard work and dedication.

Quiñones-Hinojosa was held back by a life of poverty and a lack of opportunity. In the 1980s, when he was 19, Quiñones-Hinojosa moved with his parents from Baja California, Mexico, to Fresno, California. The family immigrated illegally, so they struggled to find means by which they could survive in a new country. However, they were determined to create better lives for themselves.

Even though the work was tough, he found a job as a farm laborer in the Central Valley. That entire first year, he lived in a beat-down truck camper. The second year, the family was able to move from Fresno to Stockton where Quiñones-Hinojosa transitioned to a job loading railroad freight cars.

Though he was surviving, he knew in his heart that there was more to life than just existing as a farm laborer or freight car loader. He could see ahead of him a better future waiting to be taken hold of. Quiñones-Hinojosa took a leap of faith in hopes of improving his circumstances. He enrolled in English classes at San Joaquin Delta College. After that, he was able to enroll in general education courses. His life was finally heading somewhere, and he knew that it was the start of an incredible journey.

While Quiñones-Hinojosa was attending college, the Immigration Reform and Control Act of 1986 passed, giving him permanent legal residency in the U.S. He met his wife Anna while at college, too. A pathway to the future he wanted was being made clear to him. He gained an interest in science in those years, so he pressed on in the direction of medicine.

He was then accepted and offered a scholarship to attend University of California, Berkeley. He pursued and worked toward his dream, and in 1994, he graduated with honors. From there, he reached even higher and went to Harvard Medical School. In 1999, he graduated *cum laude* a year early.

Quiñones-Hinojosa then went on to his residency at the University of California, San Francisco.

His exemplary life shows that the "impossible" may be obtainable after all. Currently, he is a resident in Bel Air, Maryland, directs Johns Hopkins' Bayview Medical Center's brain tumor surgery program, and leads research on the role of stem cells in brain tumors and brain cancer. Now 40-years-old with three kids, he is grateful for the opportunities he has been given over the years. Dr. Alfred Quiñones-Hinojosa feels he is giving back to society for all the stepping stones it gave to him to become what he is today. He proudly says, "The world will give you the best if you give the world your best."

This article first appeared in the November, 2010, edition of the BenGlassLaw newsletter.

Chapter 22 – Dan Kennedy

Take Action To Promote Yourself, Your Ideas, Your Business, Products And Services

Some years back I had lunch with Coach Bill Foster, then in charge of the entire Southwest Conference of college basketball, after a long, incredibly distinguished coaching career. Bill gave the famous Jim Valvano his first coaching job. Bill had a phenomenal tenure at Duke and then at the University of South Carolina. *Esquire Magazine* featured him as "Dale Carnegie on the basketball court", because of his reputation as a powerful motivator. He turned Northwestern's program around. In every case, everywhere Bill went, attendance soared, alumni support increased, and community involvement with the team improved dramatically. Bottom-line: Bill Foster knows how to fill seats.

And that's what we talked about at lunch; what he was busily doing for the SWC's schools, most with sagging attendance; teaching and motivating coaches to become promoters, and relentlessly promoting. The year 'before Bill', the tournament's big Tip-Off Luncheon, for example, had only 300 in attendance; Bill's first year, 1,000; and Bill's goal for the next one, 1,500—a 500% increase in two seasons. Schools with game attendance down to 2,000 will, with a single season, climb to 4,500 with Bill's determined influence.

What Bill Foster Knows About Success That Most People Don't (Or Don't Want To)

Here's what Bill told me, that everybody needs to hear and take to heart (whether they like it or not): Coaches, he told me, *often don't understand that what they do off the basketball court, all year round, in their communities and with the national media, promoting, is as important as what they do on the court*—because, if attendance sags, the university's easiest fix is to fire the coach and bring in a new coach, with new excitement and new promises. Because, if attendance sags, recruiting suffers. Because, if attendance sags, player confidence and commitment suffers.

In other words, a very, very important part of the coach's responsibility is promotion. In other words, the "core" of coaching (like the "core" of operating a restaurant, owning a pet shop, writing books, being a jeweler, whatever) is not of sole importance; it is not the key to success. The smart coach is an assertive, creative promoter. *"One of the signs on my wall says, a terrible thing happens when you don't promote,"* Bill said, smiling. *"Nothing."*

I have watched Bill's career closely, and I'll tell you something; if you didn't know where he was, you could figure it out just by collecting and looking at the promotional literature, the calendars, the newsletters, the mailings of each school. One would stand out above all others. And that's where you'd find Bill Foster.

You see, in EVERY field of endeavor, in ANY field of endeavor, the winners are promoters.

Now, some people will want to argue about how unfair that is. I saw some clown from the American Bar Association on a talk show the other day blaming the legal profession's disfavor with the public on "those attorneys who do a lot of advertising." At Arizona State University, the academic in-crowd just about ostracized the professor who turned *"Where There's A Will, There's An 'A' "* into a giant nationwide bestseller, making himself famous and rich along the way. That's all crap. It's jealousy. Ego speaking. Those unwilling to promote are always the biggest, most vocal critics of those successful through promotion. Pick any field and you'll find both. You'll find very vocal critics of promoters. And you'll find tremendously successful promoters.

General Patton was viewed by many of his peers as a shameless, egotistical promoter. Madonna, throughout her career, has been sneered at as a no-talent self-promoter. Countless, ultimately respected and celebrated leaders in every imaginable field have risen to the mountaintop or brought themselves back from failure and disgrace via relentless, widely criticized self-promotion. And let's add the adage, *"There have been many statues erected to honor those highly criticized, but very few statues erected to critics."*

You Only Get To Choose From Door #1 or Door #2

You really have two choices. You can choose to stick your nose up at the promoters, criticize them and criticize promotion, view it as unseemly, as beneath you, as crass, and stand around grumbling about it. OR you can get good at it and use it to create influence, prominence, prestige, credibility, celebrity, career and financial success. It is your choice.

The coaches Bill works with face these choices. Some of those who choose "Door #1" will lose their current positions and move "down" to smaller schools, and there they may very well find happiness, peace of mind, a "home", and that's okay. Many, though, will move "down" and be puzzled and embittered by it. They'll live forever in envy of others they judge to be less qualified, less capable coaches than they are. The world is full of such people.

A few will pick "Door #2". *They'll get the message.* They'll somehow get intellectually and emotionally okay with the way things really are. They'll dig in and learn and adapt and grow. They'll become great promoters. And those are the coaches whose names you and I will know.

Let me now try and summarize the message.

Waiting around to be discovered, to be recognized, to be noticed, to be appointed, to be promoted guarantees one thing and one thing only: old age. Focusing on doing whatever it is that you do better than anybody else and trusting that that alone is enough (and arguing tireless that it *should* be enough) guarantees one thing and one thing only: a long life of labor in oblivion.

If Jesus had hung around his hometown working as a carpenter, giving his talks at the local Kiwanis Club meeting, writing books that never got published waiting to be discovered, we might all be Zen Buddhists today. He was a pretty bold, bombastic promoter. Turned wet bread into fish. Healed the blind. Pitched a fit about the merchants hanging around the temple. Well, you know the story. I don't have to tell you about it. You know the story because Jesus was such a great promoter.

Chapter 23 – Ben Glass

What Did Your Year Look Like?

Note: This article was first written for college students, but I find that the lessons in it are equally applicable to everyone else.

What a strange question. What DID your year look like? My editor scratched it out at first. I put it back in. Here's what I mean: close your eyes. Imagine your report card. What did your year look like? Are you happy with the way it turned out? Are your parents happy? If not, what went wrong?

Here are the top 3 reasons why 80% of all college students will express regret every May.

1. **They never sat down to really plan out the semester/year.** They took things one day at a time. Hey, you've got a syllabus. In the real world you'll never get a step-by-step guide to success typed out and handed to you!

2. **They let themselves to distracted too easily.** Sure, everyone loves a party. How about that iPhone that keeps you wired 24/7? Best thing you could do each day is find an hour where you find a quiet place "where no one knows your name," turn off all of your

doohickeys, take a blank piece of paper and just think. I DARE you to try this.

3. **They hang out with losers.** I know… this is a tough one. You don't want to "give up" on your friends, even if they sleep till 11 am and stay up till 3a.m. I'm giving you a 100% guarantee that your grades would be better and you would be happier if you started hanging out with winners. Find those people that do things bigger, better, faster and bolder than you do.

As I told the students at Christopher Newport last year, there's a reason why 80% of the world's wealth is controlled by 20% of the population and it has nothing to do with luck.

This article first appeared in the October, 2009, edition of the BenGlassLaw newsletter.

Chapter 24 – Dan Kennedy

**It's Not Enough To Act On Your Ideas.
The Only Reliable Path To Maximum
Success Is Maximum Action**

My speaking colleague Jim Rohn says that when you look closely at the highly successful individual in any field, you walk away saying to yourself: *"It's no wonder he's doing so well... look at everything he's doing."* Well, there's a darned good test! If we followed you around for a week and painstakingly recorded how you spent your time, what you did every day to advance your career or business, would we wind up saying to ourselves "It's no wonder he's doing so well—look at everything he's doing"?

The truth is that most people are intellectually lazy, surprisingly un-curious in their acquisition of information. And, in their businesses, they lazily rely on only one, two or three methods of attracting customers or clients. As a consultant, quite frankly, I do not walk away from most clients saying "It's no wonder he's doing so well look at everything he's doing." Mostly, I say to myself: "It's a miracle he's doing as well as he is—look at how little he's doing."

I once knew a chiropractor who built three million dollar a year practices. Not one, three. Dr. S. built and sold one, moved to another community, built and sold another one, and one's a fluke but three's a system, so the word spread and a whole lot of doctors wanted to know how he did that. So many, so much so, that thousands each paid $30,000.00 to come and hear him expound on his methods in seminars. But the essence of his success was really quite simple. Invariably, every doctor asked him the same question: "How can I get __ new patients this month?" How can I get 30 new patients this month? How can I get 50 new patients this month? The number varied but the question was always the same. And so was Dr. S.'s answer: *"I don't know one way to get 30 new patients, but I know 30 ways to get a new patient and I use every single one of them."*

See, if you need new clients for your business, don't do one thing, do a dozen things. If you have a problem to solve, don't implement one possible solution; implement a dozen. One of the speakers I appeared with frequently was Reverend Robert Schuller, and he's become famous for his story of how he faced the massive cost overruns in completing The Crystal Cathedral. Confronted with a need for ten million dollars, he made a list of ten different ways he might raise that money. Then he went to work on all ten simultaneously.

In my Renegade Millionaire System, I focus in depth and at length bordering on the tedious, on this important point of counter-intuitive differentiation between highly successful people and the majority. *Everyone* was taught and conditioned to do things sequentially, step by step, one thing at a time, in as orderly and organized and logical a way as possible.

The majority stick with this, the exceptionally successful—at some point—dump it by the roadside and, instead, engage in the barely controlled chaos of simultaneous initiatives, remedies and actions. They cook up success in very messy kitchens.

Take action to <u>diversify</u> the way that money and success comes to you, the way that you solve problems, even the way that you acquire new information and grow as a person.

Curiosity, incidentally, is a wonderful thing. Forget the old 'curiosity killed the cat' thing; curiosity is what uncovers opportunities and makes people rich. The average child of 5 to 10 asks hundreds of questions a day; the average adult asks only a handful. This is why kids have so much energy and enthusiasm for living. This is also why adults age prematurely and rapidly. Life-force itself comes from curiosity and creativity. *"Always Be Creating and Discovering, with Enthusiasm."* When it becomes "went there, did that", you have at least one foot in the grave.

What Kind Of Action Yields The Greatest Results?

Yes, there is one type or kind of "action" that produces maximum results in a minimum length of time, thanks in part to 'the principle of momentum.' Again, it's from Jim Rohn that I first heard about the incredibly powerful Principle Of Massive Action. The key word here is: <u>Massive</u>.

Not tiny action. Not wimpy action. Not tentative action. Not toe-in-the-water action. Not ponderously slow action. Massive action.

In 1946, a man named Walter Russell had his philosophies published, largely because he was such an unusual, larger-than-life figure. Russell never went past elementary school, and his first job was a clerk in a dry goods store earning $2.50 a week. To the amazement of just about everybody who knew of his "non-background", Russell achieved considerable fame and success as an architect, sculptor, and artist. With the publication of his success philosophies, Russell became known as "the man who tapped the secrets of the universe." Russell insisted that every man has consummate genius within, and taught that "every successful man or genius has three particular qualities in common, and the most conspicuous of these is that they all produce a prodigious amount of work."

In his classic *Lead The Field* recordings, Earl Nightingale told, with slight sarcasm, of the man who arrives home everyday and says to his family "Boy am I tired"—because that's what he heard his father say everyday when he arrived home from work, at a job, under conditions that really warranted the expression of exhaustion. I am often impressed at how little work people are willing to do in order to get what they insist they want.

Let me give you an example of the Principle Of Massive Action in action: a woman, Barbara L., cornered me at a seminar, introduced herself as the CEO of a specialized, industrial company—in her words, a woman in a man's world, and told me of her frustrations and woes with finding financing. She was literally turning away lucrative manufacturing contracts because she couldn't finance the necessary raw materials, labor and other costs while in production and then waiting to be paid a month or so following delivery. Having once run a specialty manufacturing company with similar problems, I instantly had empathy—and ideas —for her, but first I asked some questions. And I was not surprised to discover that she had tried most local banks, suffered rejection, and pretty much given up.

From my own experience, I knew Barbara had stopped at only scratching the surface of potential solutions. But she was no different than most. Most people, confronted with a problem, think of and try only a few solutions, and give up quite easily. This, incidentally, is the blunt truth behind many of our popularized societal ills and failures. Most people who "can't" get jobs actually have given up on getting a job. People who "can't" get off welfare have truthfully given up getting off of welfare. Here's why this is inarguably true: because there are people just like them who have persevered and gotten jobs, who have persevered and gotten off welfare. If one can, everyone can.

So, just as example, here was my prescription for Barbara:

THE ULTIMATE SUCCESS SECRET

1. Strengthen the proposal package and re-contact every bank that said no. Then keep re-contacting them and bringing them up-to-date every thirty days.

2. Reach out to friends, associates, community contacts, vendors in search of recommendations of other lenders and/or somebody who has a relationship of some kind with someone of authority in one of those banks.

3. Discuss different formats for the financing: revolving receivables credit line OR asset-based long term loan OR 90-day notes. Ask the banks for different things.

4. Contact banks outside the local market…draw a 300 mile circle around the plant and contact every bank in that circle.

5. Consider a sale/leaseback arrangement with a leasing company for all the equipment and furniture in the factory and offices.

6. Contact the SBA. Through the SBA, get put in touch with SBA Certified Lenders. And investigate the SBA's preferred lending services for women-owned businesses.

7. Get free help through the SBA, from SCORE (Service Corps. Of Retired Executives) for beefing up the business plan, proposal, etc.

8. Meet with key vendors and discuss creative, extended terms that could equate to the same effect as a loan or credit line. Simultaneously, open up conversations with new, alternative vendors who might use credit as a means of acquiring new business.

9. Consider factoring some receivables. Meet with factoring companies and brokers.

10. Offer customers a significant discount for paying 50% to 100% of the contracts in advance. (There is a cost of financing, no matter how you do it. You can convert that cost to a discount for prepayment without impact on true, net profit.)

11. Advertise for private lenders and "angels."

12. Form a new limited partnership or corporation with private investors, which will serve as a financing-for-profit business, lending against your other company's receivables.

13. Franchise or pseudo-franchise exclusive sales territories, and use the fees collected from that to establish your own financing fund.

14. Alter the nature of your business, the "mix" of your business, so you can get cash-with-order business.

15. Through blind, confidential advertising, put the entire business up for sale and test the waters.

16. Meet with key employees and discuss possibilities for assembling receivables financing or equity investment from employees.

Now, here's the "trick" I shared with Barbara: do all 16 of these things at the same time. Right now. Fast. Back when I ran a company with its nose pushed up against this same wall, I did all 16 of these things. In our case, we succeeded with #'s 3, 5, 8, 10 and 14. #10 alone, incidentally, dramatically altered the company's cash flow situation, even though everybody told me that the clients in our industry would never pre-pay for their manufacturing orders. In three months, we converted over half the existent clients to pre-paying, for a 10% discount.

But if we had tried one, done everything we could before giving up on one, THEN tried two, done everything we could with two, THEN tried three… it's pretty obvious that time's going to win and we're going to lose.

Of course, she might have responded—as most would—with "Geez, that's a lot of work!" And she might have said, "How am I supposed to get all that done?"… and… "But I don't know how to do all those things?"… or "I'll be working until midnight everyday to do all that." Etc. But I'm delighted to report that Barbara found an SBA Certified Lender-bank, secured a long-term loan replacing all her other financing and providing expansion capital, and she found three private individuals happy to finance individual, large receivables from new contracts as she needs them. And, it's no wonder Barbara finally got her financing; look at everything she did!

Could You Cultivate THE Most Prized Personal Characteristic Of Any And All Known To Man?

Let me give you one other example, that leads us to yet another important success behavior: in Fort Wayne, Indiana, for me, disaster struck; the set-up crew for the seminar tour called me in my hotel room, the afternoon before the event, to tell me that none of my product was at the convention center. Everyone at my office's end then did everything they thought they could do to correct the problem, to get UPS to deliver early the next day, to try and trace the location of the shipment. They did everything they *thought* they could do, but they still stopped short of doing everything that *could* be done. As concerned and earnest as they were, they stopped short. Why? Because very, very few people understand the idea of refusing to accept anything less than success.

After they gave up, I dug in. Through a series of phone calls and conversations, I finally got the guy standing on the right receiving dock, in Ft. Wayne, Indiana. I sold him—and I mean: *sold*—on getting up early the next morning, getting to his warehouse, and going through the carloads of boxes left there during the night to find mine. And to call me by

7:00 AM that morning with the good news that he had done so. And, a little after 7:00 AM, he was on the phone. And he had the boxes loaded in his own, personal pick-up truck. And he brought them to the convention center, undoubtedly in violation of a handful of company regulations. And, for you cynics, I didn't offer him money, he never asked for money, and when we finally tried to give him money that morning, he refused it. Now, I honestly believe that I did not do anything here that anybody else couldn't have done. This was not a matter of "talent." I just refused to accept anything less than success. I stayed at it long enough and hard enough that I got a little "earned luck", and found a guy like me – two people who can and will "carry the message to Garcia." If you don't know the story of the man who carried the message to Garcia, I've reprinted it here. It reveals the most prized characteristic on earth.

A Message To Garcia

In all this Cuban business there is one man stands out on the horizon of my memory like Mars at perihelion.

When war broke out between Spain and the United States, it was very necessary to communicate quickly with the leader of the Insurgents. Garcia was somewhere in the mountain vastness of Cuba – no one knew where. The President must secure his cooperation, and quickly.

What to do!

Someone said to the President, "There is a fellow by the name of Rowan will find Garcia for you, if anybody can."

Rowan was sent for and given a letter to be delivered to Garcia. How the "fellow by the name of Rowan" took the letter, sealed it up in an oilskin pouch, strapped it over his heart, in four days landed by night off the cost of Cuba from an open boat, disappeared on the other side of the Island, having traversed a hostile country on foot, and delivered his letter to Garcia—are things I have no special desire now to tell in detail. The point that I wish to make is this: McKinley gave Rowan a letter to be delivered to Garcia; Rowan took the letter and did not ask, "Where is he at?"

By the Eternal! there is a man whose form should be cast in deathless bronze and the statue placed in every college of the land. It is not book-learning young men need, nor instruction about this and that, but a stiffening of the vertebrae which will cause them to be loyal to a trust, to act promptly, concentrate their energies: do the thing "Carry a message to Garcia."

General Garcia is dead now, but there are other Garcias. No man who has endeavored to carry out an enterprise where many hands were needed, but has been well-nigh appalled at times by the imbecility of the average man – the inability or unwillingness to concentrate on a thing and do it.

Slipshod assistance, foolish inattention, dowdy indifference, and half-hearted work seem the rule; and no man succeeds, unless by hook or crook or threat he forced or bribes other men to assist him; or mayhap, God in His goodness performs a miracle, and sends him an Angel of Light for an assistant.

You, reader, put this matter to a test: You are sitting now in your office—six clerks are within call. Summon any one and make this request: "Please look in the encyclopedia and make a brief memorandum for me concerning the life of Correggio."

Will the clerk quietly say, "Yes, sir," and go do the task?

On your life he will not. He will look at you out of a fishy eye and ask one or more of the following questions:

Who was he?

Which encyclopedia?

Where is the encyclopedia?

Was I hired for that?

Don't you mean Bismarck?

What's the matter with Charlie doing it?

Is he dead?

Is there any hurry?

Sha'n't I bring you the book and let you look it up yourself?

What do you want to know for?

And I will lay you ten to one that after you have answered the questions, and explained how to find the information, and why you want it, the clerk will go off and get one of the other clerks to help him try to find Garcia—and then come back and tell you there is no such man. Of course I may lose my bet, but according to the Law Of Average I will not.

Now, if you are wise, you will not bother to explain to your "assistant" that Correggio is indexed under the C's, not in the K's, but you will smile very sweetly and say, "Never mind," and go look it up yourself. And this incapacity for independent action, this moral stupidity, this infirmity of the will, this unwillingness to cheerfully catch hold and lift – these are the things that put pure Socialism so far into the future. If men will not act for themselves, what will they do when the benefit of their effort is for all?

A fist mate with knotted club seems necessary; and the dread of getting "the bounce" Saturday night holds many a worker to his place. Advertise for a stenographer, and nine out of ten who apply can neither spell nor punctuate – and do not think it necessary to.

Can such a one write a letter to Garcia?

"You see that bookkeeper," said the foreman to me in a large factory.

"Yes; what about him?"

"Well, he's a fine accountant, but if I'd send him up town on an errand, he might accomplish the errand all right, and on the other hand, might stop at four saloons on the way, and when he got to Main Street would forget what he had been sent for."

Can such a man be entrusted to carry a message to Garcia?

We have recently been hearing much maudlin sympathy expressed for the "downtrodden denizens of the sweatshop" and the "homeless wanderer searching for honest employment," and with it all often go many hard words for the men in power.

Nothing is said about the employer who grows old before his time in a vain attempt to get frowzy ne'er-do-wells to do intelligent work; and his long, patient striving after "help" that does nothing but loaf when his back is turned. In every store and factory there is a constant weeding-out process going on. The employer is constantly sending away "help" that have shown their incapacity to further the interests of the business, and others are being taken on. No matter how good times are, this sorting continues: only, if times are hard and work is scarce, the sorting is done finer—but out and forever out the incompetent and unworthy go. It is the survival of the fittest. Self-interest prompts every employer to keep the best—those who can carry a message to Garcia.

I know one man of really brilliant parts who has not the ability to manage a business of his own, and yet who is absolutely worthless to anyone else, because he carries with him constantly the insane suspicion that his employer is oppressing, or intending to oppress, him. He cannot give orders, and he will not receive them. Should a message be given him, to take to Garcia, his answer would probably be, "Take it yourself!"

Tonight this man walks the streets looking for work, the wind whistling through his threadbare coat. No one who knows him dare employ him, for he is a regular firebrand of discontent. He is impervious to reason, and the only thing that can impress him is the toe of a thick-soled Number Nine boot.

Of course, I know that one so morally deformed is no less to be pitied than a physical cripple; but in our pitying let us drop a tear, too, for the men who are striving to carry on a great enterprise, whose working hours are not limited by the whistle, and whose hair is fast turning white through the struggle to hold in line dowdy indifference, slipshod imbecility, and the heartless ingratitude which, but for their enterprise, would be both hungry and homeless.

Have I put the matter too strongly? Possibly I have; but when all the world has done a-slumming I wish to speak a word of sympathy for the man who succeeds – the man who, against great odds, has directed the efforts of others, and having succeeded, finds there's nothing in it: nothing but bare board and clothes. I have carried a dinner-pail and worked for a day's wages, and I have also been an employer of labor, and I know there is something to be said on both sides. There is no excellence, per se, in poverty; rags are no recommendation; and all employers are not rapacious and high-handed, any more than all poor men are virtuous. My heart goes out to the man who does his work when the "boss" is away, as well as when he is at home. And the man who, when given a letter for Garcia, quietly takes the missive, without asking any idiotic questions, and with no lurking intention of chucking it into the nearest sewer, or of doing naught else but deliver it, never gets "laid off," nor has to go on a strike for higher wages. Civilization is one long, anxious search for just such individuals. Anything such a man asks shall be granted. He is wanted in every city, town and village —in every office, shop, store and factory. The world cries out for such; he is needed and needed badly—the man who can "Carry a Message to Garcia."

Chapter 25 – Ben Glass

Never Give Up

I'm amazed at the little things that will keep some people from maximizing their gifts and talents.

Things like getting up on time to get to class. Like not being able to find the information they need for a project immediately when there's a library—with real librarians—within biking distance who can help you find and hold real books. Losers.

I love reading about hugely successful people who never should have been a success because they got dealt a raw deal. (No, I'm not talking about not getting into your number one choice for college. That's not a raw deal. That's not a rip-off. I'm tired of hearing parents whine about how tough it is for kids today. Don't get me going.)

Did you ever read the story of the founder of Kinko's, Pau Orfalea? Described as a hyperactive dyslexic, he saw a line of people at a new fangled photocopy machine one day and saw an opportunity. Built a $2 billion (yes, billion with a B) company out of an opportunity. Didn't invent some new whizbang computer operating system. Didn't revolutionize the world with a new techno-gadget. Orfalea saw a way to serve people better.

More recently, Inc. Magazine profiled Alison Schuback. Betcha never heard of her, either. I'm guessing no college professor in America spends a day showing kids what makes her tick. This 23-year-old working on a master's degree has her world turned upside down in a car accident. Pretty bad brain injury. A tailor-made excuse for packing it in and calling it a life.

Not wanting to rely on a bailout to pay her own medical bills, she saw a need and invented a transparent, washable bib for adults with disabilities. She pitched it to some companies and, BINGO, she's leading a company of 100 employees who are making and selling the bib. (It certainly helped that her parents were entrepreneurial and probably constantly whispered in her ear, from the time that she was little, that NOTHING is impossible in America.)

This article first appeared in the June, 2009, edition of the BenGlassLaw newsletter.

Chapter 26 – Dan Kennedy

Take Action To Turn Failure Into Success

I once saw a particularly ornery dog latch onto a mailman's leg. The mailman shook his leg but the dog held on, growling menacingly. The mailman kicked the dog with his other leg.

The dog held on. The mailman drug the dog down the sidewalk. The dog held on. The mailman sprayed the dog with Mace. He hit the dog on the head with his mail sack.

He swung his leg, dog attached, into a tree trunk. The dog held on. I thought to myself: there is the dog version of Dan Kennedy.

In his best-selling book, *Swim With The Sharks,* Harvey MacKay tells of being turned down by all his local lending institutions. Then he drew a 3-inch circle on the map around his city and called on all the banks within that circle. They all turned him down too. He drew a bigger circle. Eventually he got his loan. He says he'd still be drawing ever-bigger circles if he hadn't connected. I believe him.

If you look at most highly successful entrepreneurs, you won't find markedly superior talent, intelligence, education or resources. Self-made millionaires are surprisingly ordinary—and, often, surprisingly unintelligent—people.

Conversely, a small percentage of Mensa members are self-made millionaires. So it ain't intelligence. Instead it seems to have much to do with a profound sort of stubbornness.

How You Deal With Failure Determines Whether Or Not You Ever Get To Deal With Success

Research supervised by a professor at Tulane University revealed that the average entrepreneur goes through 3.8 failures before achieving significant success.

Actually, the entire entrepreneurial experience is one of frequent failure interrupted by occasional success. The entire experience of selling is one of frequent refusal (rejection) interrupted by occasional acceptance. In direct marketing, we call it "testing", not failure. But a whole lot more "tests" fail than succeed.

Go Ahead, Screw Up, Fall Down. Embarrass Yourself. A Lot. Fast.

There IS value in making mistakes. General Schwarzkopf discussed one situation he encountered where, if a bundle of decisions were made and actions taken and 49% turned out wrong, everybody'd still be way ahead of where they were with no decisions being made and no actions taken. I say: screw up. Fall down. The opposite requires living in constant fear of error, and that's a sad, pitiful existence. You have to look at every significant accomplishment as the end result of a certain number of successes but also a certain number of failures.

When I first wrote this book, Billy Crystal was one of Hollywood's hottest comic actors. His movie *City Slickers* was a huge hit, birthing a sequel. But his movie *Mr. Saturday Night,* which he deeply believed in, was Dead On Arrival at theaters. Almost every top-earning actor or movie producer has flops and failures and downs as well as ups. If you can find the made-for-cable autobiographical films *His Way*, by and about Jerry Weintraub, and *A Piece Of Work*, about Joan Rivers, I urge getting them and viewing them, for raw, candid, dramatic demonstrations of rise, fall and rise again.

Sinatra was once dropped by his record label, judged "washed up." Disneyland's live-televised grand opening was a comedy of errors, reported on by media as "a disaster", "not ready for prime time" and a place "not worth paying to visit." Ouch. And ouch again.

If you aren't willing to risk actions that may cause you personal, financial or other embarrassment, you aren't going to be taking much action at all. So go ahead: screw up, fall down, embarrass yourself, and do a lot of it, as quickly as you can. Learn as much as you possibly can as you go. But, whatever you do, don't let yourself be imprisoned by the fear of making mistakes.

Death Of An Actor

One of the saddest stories ever to come out of Hollywood was the rather sordid tale of the death of a young actor named Barry Brown. He played leading roles in *Bad Company and Daisy Miller,* and he was an actor of unusual promise. But he had the misfortune to do his best work in movies that were, in one way or another, unsuccessful. As he found it increasingly difficult to get parts, he became depressed, began drinking heavily and behaving erratically. He was found in his home, shot thorough the head with a gun and bottle beside him, and friends theorized he had been playing Russian roulette and had not intended suicide.

Barry Brown, dead at 27, had talent, looks and intelligence. All he lacked was the one quality that, if absent, can make the rest useless: he lacked the ability to hang in, the emotional strength necessary to reject rejection and keep coming back for more.

It is the same in many professions, of course. "From salesman to saxophonist, the individual who risks something of himself in performance has to be somewhat inured to rebuff.

So wrote Bruce Cook, contributing editor to *American Film Magazine,* in an article for *The Wall Street Journal* a few years ago.

This story is all the more tragic when you consider that it must be representative of tens of thousands of similar stories, some reported, some not, of people who gave up.

It's such stories that prove that talent, genius, and education are no assurances of success. In fact, the history of American business is full of stories of people lacking in those qualities but strong in persistence who have achieved the incredible.

One has to wonder how much greater America would be as a nation, in all respects, if the best and the brightest were also the most persistent.

Probably the best thing about being in business for yourself is that there isn't anybody to give a letter of resignation to when the going gets tough. Industrialist C.F. Kettering said, "No one ever would have crossed the ocean if he could have gotten off the ship in the storm."

I can think of a number of times when I've wanted to quit and didn't, mostly because I couldn't.

In my experience, far more business success comes purely from persistence than from invention or investment. There's a lot to be said for simply not giving up.

(Note: Portions of the above reprinted from the book "Kennedy On Money/Business/Success, © 1985.)

So, How DO You Convert Failure to Success?

First, just by hanging in. Quite often, failure transforms itself to success purely as a result of persistence. Ernest Hemingway reportedly rewrote the *Old Man And The Sea* two hundred times and tried forty-four different endings for *A Farewell To Arms*. Keep trying a slightly different approach. But keep trying.

The insightful writer Ben Stein says, "<u>Failure is like a patient teacher</u> who tells us, 'No, THAT won't work. Try it a little differently. Or maybe a lot differently.' If you look at failure as a coach, as a manager encouraging you to try different approaches, you get a much better idea of what failure is."

Second, by diligently looking for the concealed opportunity. To quote proverbs and adages: nothing is either as good or as bad as it fist appears to be... and... whenever one door closes, another opens. Personally, every great disaster, disappointment and tragedy in my life has directly led to a greater opportunity or benefit. Every single time. But, you can only find what you look for, see what you expect to see.

Are there exceptions? I suppose so. There ARE some "failures" in which I've been unable to uncover any IMMEDIATE benefit or opportunity—and those, set aside as "unfinished business" (rather than "*permanent* failure") have, in time, yielded enormous value. But these exceptions are few and far between.

Third, by taking prompt, decisive, constructive action. *Stopping* is the absolute worst thing that you can do. I wonder how many shots Michael Jordan MISSED (failures!) in his pro basketball career? Even how many CRUCIAL shots he missed? Well, one thing's certain; when he did miss one, he didn't rush over to the bench, get the coach to take him out of the game, sit down on the bench, put a towel over his head, and refuse to take another shot for the rest of the game. What did he do when he missed? As soon as possible, he took another shot. Cotton Fitzsimmons, a wise, veteran coach, now in management with the Phoenix Suns says "Sometimes you have to let a player just shoot his way out of a slump." No, *stopping* is not the answer. Instead, as with most problems, action is the only true antidote.

Epilogue

By now, you should have "locked in" on the Ultimate Success Secret presented to you a number of times throughout this book. The people who are LIVING this Secret are the most respected and admired, influential and powerful, successful and happy individuals on the planet.

I would like to add a very brief discussion about just one *application* of this Secret—and to quickly note that, like all advice, it's easier said than done; that, like "the fat doctor", I could stand to take my own medicine more frequently; but that does not diminish the importance of the ideas.

On the long, often dangerously boring drive from Phoenix to Las Vegas, there are signs posted frequently, at sites of deadly accidents, warning drivers not to drive if they've been drinking, not to drive if fatigued. The signs say:

THERE IS A

LAST TIME

FOR

EVERYTHING.

Tell your wife (or husband) you love her (or him) more often. And especially tell her (or him) *today*, because they might be gone tomorrow. There is a last time for everything.

Stop and have a friendly conversation with your Mom, Dad, a friend, the guy at the newsstand on the corner. Take just a few minutes for this more often than you do. And, especially *today*. They might be gone tomorrow. There is a last time for everything.

I called to talk to a friend the other day, another entrepreneur as busy, as obsessed as I; she wasn't in; when she called back she said, almost apologetically, and wryly, "I was out having a Life." She had gone out to lunch with someone 100% unrelated to her business. Whatever it is that you really, really enjoy doing, really, really, really enjoy it the next time you do it. There is a last time for everything.

When you go to your job or place of business today, be thankful you've got one, and give it the very best you've got. Tomorrow, thousands will lose their jobs—and *then*, maybe, wish they'd done things there differently. Tomorrow, a thousand entrepreneurs will close business' doors—and *then*, maybe, wonder what might have happened if they'd advertised more creatively, sold more aggressively. There is a last time for everything.

Whatever you're going to do today, give it your best, and take from it the best you can. There is a last time for everything.

THERE'S A LAST TIME FOR EVERYTHING

Just Do It.
—Nike

About The Authors

Ben Glass is a practicing attorney in Fairfax, VA. He has authored numerous consumer guides, including *The Five Deadly Sins That Can Wreck Your Injury Claim*, *Robbery Without a Gun*, and *Why Most Medical Malpractice Victims Never Recover a Dime*. Ben is a national authority on the subject of attorney marketing and has gained acclaim for applying marketing tactics from many other fields to the legal profession, even when others said it couldn't be done. His legal marketing company, Great Legal Marketing, coaches hundreds of attorneys across the nation, in addition to putting on a number of conferences that draw sold-out crowds every year. You can order the official Great Legal Marketing book at GreatLegalMarketingBook.com

Ben resides in Northern Virginia with his wife Sandi and 9 kids (four of whom he adopted from China through the organization Love Without Boundaries). For the past 5 years, Ben has run the Marine Corps Marathon on behalf of Love Without Boundaries and serves on the board.

Dan Kennedy is a multi-millionaire serial entrepreneur, celebrated author of numerous books published in the U.S. and abroad (in translated editions) and recognized by *INC.*, *Entrepreneur*, *Forbes* and other leading publications, and a sought after consultant and direct marketing strategist. He is the editor of *The No B.S. Marketing Letter* and five other professional newsletters. As a speaker, he has repeatedly appeared on programs with leading business and success speakers including Zig Ziglar, Brian Tracy and Tom Hopkins, as well as numerous celebrity entrepreneurs including Gene Simmons (KISS), Donald Trump, Ivanka Trump, Debbi Fields (Mrs. Fields Cookies), George Foreman and Joan Rivers, as well as four former U.S. Presidents and other world leaders. The organization he originated and continues contributing to as content provider and advisor, Glazer-Kennedy Insider's Circle™, now literally spans the globe, directly serves about 25,000 members, additionally distributes business information through hundreds of thought-leaders in diverse industries, has local Chapters meeting in many cities, and conducts two major marketing-oriented conferences a year. Information about the author's books and activities may be accessed at www.NoBSBooks.com. Direct communication with the author should be done via fax: 602/269-3113. (E-mail to any of his publishers' web sites will not receive personal attention or response.) Mr. Kennedy is available for a very limited number of interesting and appropriate speaking, consulting, writing or direct-response copywriting engagements each year.

Mr. Kennedy lives in Ohio and Virginia, with his 2nd and 3rd wife (one in the same) and The Million Dollar Dog, although his office is in Arizona. He owns a stable of Standardbred racehorses and personally drives professionally in over 200 races a year, most at Northfield Park. Races can be seen at NorthfieldPark.com or on the cable TV network TVG.

About This Book

This book is a product of Pete-The-Printer.com, and it, along with several other special-purpose Dan Kennedy books, are available in bulk quantities or licensed, for re-publishing and or co-authorship or anthology publishing. Inquiries should be directed to Pete Lillo at Pete-The-Printer.com or 330-922-9833. Pete-The-Printer.com/Pete Lillo & Associates is also the publisher of Dan Kennedy's *Look Over My Shoulder* Newsletter for direct-response copywriters and direct marketers.

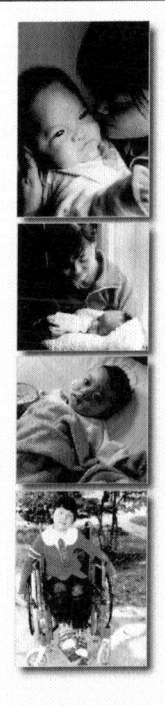

GIVE HOPE *AND* HEALING *TO A CHILD IN NEED*

Ben Glass serves on the board of Love Without Boundaries, a non-profit organization dedicated to saving the lives of orphaned and impoverished children in China. LWB's vision is to provide the most loving and compassionate help possible to these children, and to show the world that every child, regardless of his or her needs, deserves to experience love and be treated with dignity and care. As a Board Member, Ben has the privilege of "meeting" children every day who benefit from LWB's programs. He is always humbled by the hurdles they have overcome in their short lives.

Ben would like to invite you to become a part of these children's stories. By making a donation to help change their lives you can make a positive difference in the world.

For more information on any of their programs, please visit www.LoveWithoutBoundaries.com *or email them at* info@lwbmail.com.

Donations can be made online or mailed to
Love Without Boundaries
PO Box 25016
Oklahoma City, OK 73125
405-216-5837

LWB is a registered 501(c)(3) charity.
100% of your charitable contributions are tax deductible in the U.S.

On behalf of all of the children in LWB programs— Ben sends his deepest thanks for your kindness and commitment toward helping those in need.

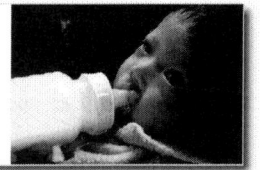

LOVE WITHOUT BOUNDARIES

Love Without Boundaries Foundation is a worldwide group of volunteers dedicated to improving the lives of orphaned and impoverished children in China by providing humanitarian aid in five key areas — Education, Foster Care, Healing Homes, Medical, and Orphanage Assistance — and enabling children to receive families through adoption or to become self-sustaining members of their communities.

WWW.LOVEWITHOUTBOUNDARIES.COM

WA